$$\frac{J \circ}{4 \cdot 99}$$

Air Spectaculars

Air Displays in Ireland

Madeleine O'Rourke

Glendale

First published in Ireland by
GLENDALE
1 Summerhill Parade
Sandycove,
Co. Dublin, Ireland

British Library Cataloguing in Publication Data

O'Rourke, Madeleine
    Air spectaculars
    1. Ireland. Air displays, history
    I. Title
    629.13'074'02916

    ISBN 0-907606-57-1

Cover by David L. Murphy
Typeset by Wendy A. Commins, The Curragh
Make-up by Paul Bray Studio
Printed by The Camelot Press, Southampton

Contents

Acknowledgements

I would like to thank the many people who have helped me in preparing this book, in particular those who gave me their time to relate wonderful memories of air displays past and present. *Weston Displays*: Chris Bruton, Maurice Cronin, Denis Greene, Ciaran McLoughlin, Pat Ward, Ernie Verso. *Early Parachuting Days*: Freddie Bond. *Limerick Displays*: Paddy Duggan, Michael Traynor. *Cobham Displays*: Pearse Cahill, Michael Cobham. *Ballooning & Gliding Displays*: David Hooper.

Thanks also to: Brian Byrne, Eddy Carroll, Jimmy Condon, Mick Donoghue, Stanley Dunne, D.H. Gillman, John Grey, Kathleen Malone, William Malpas, Alex McAllister, Brigadier General Brian McMahon, Ken Mellor, Liam Murphy, Lt. Col. M. O'Malley, R.W. O'Sullivan, David Ogilvy.

For memories of Air Spectacular I wish to thank: Paddy Byrne, Johnny Carroll, Tom Farrington, Tom Garvan, Richard Goode, Tom Hudson, Anthony Hutton, Peter Hynes, Mike Kelly, Dr. Colm and Ita Killeen, Brian Lecomber, Christopher Martin, Oliver McCann, Judith McClean, Liam McCobb, Liam McNulty, Kevin Myres, Brendan O'Brien, Lt. Col. John O'Brien, Ronan Power, Terry Rowan, Ken Townsend, Wing Commander Ken Wallis, Joss Yates.

For photographs I am grateful to: Aer Lingus, Alan Cobham Estate, Robert Allen, British Embassy, Liam Byrne Collection, Derek Byrne, Capt. Kevin Byrne, Air Corps Photographic Section, *Cork Examiner* Photo Library, Tony Coyne, Department of Defence, Paul Duffy Collection, George Flood Collection, *Irish Press*, *Irish Times* Photo Section, A.P. Kearns Collection, Anton Mazer, Tom McCormack, Joe Murphy Air Corps Photographic Section, Sean Murphy, David Tracey Collection.

For archival and research material I wish to thank: Paul Cunniffe, Karl Hayes (Irish Air Letter), Tommy Cranitch, Bob Harris, Dick Killen (Irish Aviation Museum), Comdt Peter Young and Staff (Army Archives), staff of National and Pearse Street Libraries, Paul Williams (Pembrokeshire Aviation Group), Gordon M. Kniveton (Manx Aviation). Thanks also to Liam Byrne who encouraged me to write this book and to Paul Duffy for proof reading the manuscript and for giving me access to his vast aviation photographic collection.

I am deeply grateful to my husband Colm for the long hours at the computer keyboard preparing the manuscript and for giving me every encouragement to complete it.

Finally, the opinions expressed in this book are my own and do not necessarily reflect the views of the Irish Aviation Council or other official bodies.

The publishers wish to acknowledge the support of Aer Rianta, Rothmans, Aer Arran, Irish Dunlop and Smirnoff in the production of this book.

To Colm and Marguerite

List of Illustrations

1
In the Beginning

Richard Crosbie

Man has been fascinated since time began with the air around him and has tried in many ways to become a part of it. If he could not participate himself he was doubly intrigued by the airmen who ventured aloft from earliest times and balloon ascents in the early days were assured of large numbers of fascinated spectators. The more enterprising of the airmen would advertise the event well in advance and hope to recoup some of the expenses by making an admission charge on the day. So was born the display spectator.

The first major aerial event, witnessed by 20,000 Irish spectators, was by the Wicklow balloonist Richard Crosbie. He ascended in his hydrogen balloon from the grounds of Ranelagh Gardens, Dublin on 19 January 1785 to become the first aeronaut ever to fly in Ireland. He landed safely shortly afterwards at Clontarf.

Other flights were attempted in May by Richard McGwire who landed in the sea seven miles north east of Howth and by a Frenchman, Dr. Portain, who ascended from Marlborough Green, Dublin on 17 June landing just north of Roundwood. He had hoped to cross the Irish Sea but the winds had other ideas. 1785 was a remarkable year which firmly established ballooning in the minds of Irish people. The balloon craze was growing and the Lord Mayor of Dublin James Horan declared that the citizens were spending too much time gaping at balloon ascents when they should be at work. In a press notice he declared his intention of preventing such events in as far as his power would permit.

In spite of the Lord Mayor's unsporting gesture Richard Crosbie planned a flight to cross the Irish Sea by hydrogen balloon. The Duke of Leinster gave him permission to use his lawns beside Leinster House (now Dàil Éireann) in Dublin for the launch site. Crosbie advertised that the attempt would be made with the first fair wind after Sunday 17 July 1785 and notice of the launch would be given by firing cannons and by beating drums two hours before the ascent. On Tuesday 19 July the wind was favourable in direction but squally. Crowds quickly gathered after the cannon fire and Crosbie ascended at 2.20 pm. Rising slowly the balloon struck a high wall enclosing the lawn and touched down in a field opposite Merrion Square before finally rising clear.

Crosbie crossed the coast and was soon out of sight. Descending in mid-channel to catch as he thought a faster current of air Crosbie found himself caught in a hail shower with strong downdraughts. Having exhausted his supply of ballast on his spectacular take off Crosbie was carried down to sea level and could not recover altitude. A ship from Dun Laoghaire rescued both pilot and balloon and brought them safely back to Ireland. He was entertained to breakfast by the Duke and Duchess of Rutland at Blackrock House. When the crowds got word of where he was they invaded the house and carried him in triumph to his home in Cumberland Street near the Rotunda hospital.

Richard Crosbie made further public ascents. One was on 27 April 1786 when he rose above Limerick city, crossed the river Shannon and landed near Ennis. As in Dublin the crowds went wild at such a magnificent demonstration. Thereafter no further flights are recorded by Ireland's first aeronaut and display pilot and he was soon to leave Ireland. He died in 1800. His burial place is unfortunately not known.

The Irish Sea was finally crossed by Windham Sadler on 22 July 1817 thirty two years after the intrepid Crosbie first headed towards Wales. He ascended from Portobello Barracks in Dublin and landed near the town of Holyhead in north Wales. In the same year Ireland's first female aerial passenger Miss Thompson, was carried aloft in a balloon piloted by Mr. Livingston. An historic occasion and the place once again was Dublin. Livingston made other ascents including one from Portobello Barracks on 22 June 1822 landing in the sea just off Baldoyle where he was rescued by boat. He donated the entire proceeds from the event to the suffering poor of the south and west of Ireland. The country was now on the threshold of the tragic potato famine which was to decimate the population by starvation and emigration.

Various other balloon ascents took place but the most spectacular was by Percival Spencer in 1889. He proclaimed that he would ascend to 5,000 ft. and then leap from the unmanned balloon and descend safely with the aid of a parachute in sight of the spectators. The gates of Clonturk Park in Drumcondra, Dublin were opened on 21 September, three hours before the ascent, to give the crowds a chance to see the preparations. A military band was engaged to add to the festive atmosphere. The admission charge was one shilling (five new pence) for the general area and three shillings and sixpence for the reserved balloon enclosure. Quite a huge sum in 1889. According to the records of the day thousands willingly paid to see this unique event. They were rewarded by Spencer's successful balloon ascent followed by his safe parachute landing only 400 yds. from his take off point. Conditions were obviously calm to allow this to happen. His balloon was ballasted at the top so that when his weight was removed from the bottom it inverted, the gas escaped and the balloon descended to a safe landing a short distance away. This was not the first parachute jump in Ireland for just one week earlier the same Mr. Spencer had made Irish aviation history by jumping from a height of 2,000 ft. on 14 September 1889 also at Clonturk Park.

On 17 December 1903 two American bicycle manufacturers, Orville and Wilbur Wright made the first powered flight in a heavier than air machine at Kitty Hawk beach, North Carolina. Orville Wright covered a distance of 120 ft. in twelve seconds. From this dramatic moment the balloon feats faded into history and the attention of the world was focussed on a brand new machine, the aeroplane, and on those daring pilots who controlled it. Few could have foreseen that this simple mechanical bird would quickly change the world.

JUMP FROM A BALLOON
On SATURDAY NEXT, 21st SEPT.,
At 5 o'Clock, p.m., in
Clonturk Park, Drumcondra.
MR. PERCIVAL SPENCER,
Of Indian Celebrity,
Will Ascend in a Balloon to the Height of about FIVE THOUSAND FEET, or ONE MILE, and
LEAP FROM THE CLOUDS
Descending safely, by means of a Parachute, in sight of the Spectators.
GATES OPEN AT 2 P.M.,
In order to give Visitors an opportunity of witnessing the interesting process of Inflating the Balloon, and watching the departure of the Pilot and Grotesque Figure Balloons.
MILITARY BAND.
Price of Admission - ONE SHILLING,
RESERVED BALLOON ENCLOSURE   -   - 3/6
CHILDREN HALF PRICE.

2 Percival Spencer

The first flight in England took place on 16 October 1908 when S.F. Cody flew for a distance of 496 yds. at a height of about fifty feet over Laffan's plain, Aldershot.

By July 7 1909 the long distance record had reached 159 miles in a time of 3 hours and 39 minutes. This was set by Olieslagers at Reims, flying a Bleriot. On 11 July the height record for Britain went up to 2,490 ft. Armstrong Drexel was the pilot. Drexel and Harry Delacombe flew the first cross country passenger flight in Great Britain, flying a two seater Bleriot from Bournemouth to Beaulieu in Hampshire, on 19 July 1909. The English Channel was crossed for the first time by Frenchman, Louis Bleriot on Sunday, 25 July 1909. It took thirty seven minutes. Aviation had come to Britain. It had an amazing effect on the British and they flocked to France to learn how to fly. Aviation history was being re-written at a furious pace, with records set and broken by the week. In August 1909 the first organised aviation meet was held at Rheims in France over the course of a week the 22nd to the 29th. There were many crashes and twelve damaged aircraft littered the airfield at one stage. Thirty eight machines were seen in the air.

Irishmen were not far behind in getting into the air using this new mode of transport. Harry Ferguson a motor car dealer from Dromore, Co. Down had visited the Reims meet in August 1909. When he got home he began the construction of an aircraft of his own. After much experiment Ferguson succeeded in making the first aeroplane flight in Ireland. This was at Hillsborough, Co. Down. He reached a height of ten feet and covered a distance of one hundred yards. The date was 31 December 1909. He went on to fly longer distances using the six mile stretch of Magilligan Strand, at the mouth of Lough Foyle, and had increased the flight distance to two and a half miles by mid-summer 1910.

On one of these later flights, in August 1910, he carried Miss Rita Marr, from Liverpool, who thus became Ireland's first aeroplane passenger.

In October 1910 he had a serious accident at Magilligan Strand. This may have diverted his attention to automobile design and construction. In this area he achieved distinction and wealth. He died in October 1960 aged seventy six, a millionnaire who had made his fortune with the Ferguson tractor. A replica of his Ferguson monoplane was constructed by the late Jack C. Kelly Rogers and contains the original JPA 35HP V8 air cooled engine and pilot's seat. This aircraft is in the care of the Irish Aviation Museum.

Spurred on by all this aeronautical activity a meeting of interested parties was held on 5 November 1909 in the meeting rooms of the Royal Irish Automobile Club in Dawson Street, Dublin and the Aero Club of Ireland was formed. The Irish Aviation Council of today is the direct descendant of this club.

Notable people of the time who attended the meeting included Harry Ferguson, Sir Henry Grattan-Bellew, J.T.C. Moore-Brabazon, later to become Lord Brabazon of Tara (first UK citizen to be issued with a pilot's licence), and John Boyd Dunlop, inventor of the pneumatic tyre. John Dunville, who was elected chairman, was to make further aviation history in February 1910 when he crossed the Irish Sea in his hydrogen balloon, starting from Ringsend, Dublin and landing during a snowstorm in Birtles, near Macclesfield, Cheshire, in a time of five hours. A remarkable feat and it was only the second time that this sea crossing had been made in ninety three years. He reached a maximum altitude of 10,000 ft.

The Aero Club of Ireland set out to encourage aerial navigation by holding aviation meetings and aerial displays for the public. The committee resolved to invite the most skilled aviators available to come to Ireland to

3 Programme page, Ireland's first Air Display, 1910

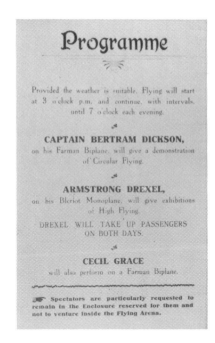

4 Programme cover, Air Display 1910

5 Captain Bertram Dickson

demonstrate their flying machines. They opened a guarantee list and raised over £2,000. Leopardstown Racecourse, Co. Dublin was selected as Ireland's first air display venue. The grass racetracks became the runways and the grandstands and other facilities were ready made for public assembly. They paid £200 for the use of the course for 29 and 30 August 1910. The invited aviators were Capt. Bertram Dickson who was paid £500 to give a demonstration of circular flying in his Farman biplane, Armstrong Drexel who would demonstrate high flying in his Bleriot monoplane for a fee of £250 and Cecil Grace who would perform in his Farman biplane for the same amount. This was big money for 1910 but the aircraft were still far from reliable and required much skill. The high fees reflected the level of risk involved. The pilots and their machines were still pioneering the art of flight and all time spent aloft was true test flying, the feedback being used to further develop the aircraft.

Bertram Dickson had served in the South African War as an Artillery Officer. Subsequently he had learned to fly at the Farman School at Mourmelon near Reims in France. He bought a Farman machine and flew at aviation meets in France. He distinguished himself as an able aviator and excelled at gliding his machine and landings. At the Angers meet in France he won most of the prizes, much to the chagrin of the French. At Rouen he won the long distance prize.

Armstrong Drexel, an American, spent much of his time in Europe and learned to fly a Bleriot monoplane at Graham White's School at Pau,

France, in 1909. He went to England in the Spring of 1910 and opened an aerodrome at Beaulieu, Hampshire, with his partner, W.F. MacArdle. A few days before coming to Leopardstown he set a new British height record of 2,490 ft. at Bournemouth.

Cecil Grace's parents emigrated from Ireland to America when his father was thirty and became American citizens. They subsequently moved to Valparaiso, Chile. Cecil was born in Valparaiso, where his father had set up a successful business. In England he took up flying in 1909, learning on Moore-Brabazon's Voisin biplane "The Bird of Passage". This was a process of trial and error: the machine was crashed and repaired many times during testing. He later acquired a Short biplane, based on the Henry Farman biplane design and modified by Roger Sumner. Sunmer built his second such machine for Grace in June 1910. Grace did a number of flights over the sea in this aircraft, including a flight over the fleet at anchor in Sheerness Harbour at the mouth of the River Thames, near London. Grace's cousin Sir Valentine Grace lived in Monkstown, Co. Dublin and Cecil stayed with him for the week of the Leopardstown display.

By the Friday before the Leopardstown meeting, the grounds had been prepared. Hangars had been erected to house the machines, which had arrived from England at the North Wall packed in wooden crates a couple of days before. These were now uncrated and assembled. Drexel's two

6 Leopardstown 1910, (left to right) Harold Perrin, Secretary Royal Aero Club, Armstrong Drexel, Harry Delacombe, W.F. MacArdle, Cecil Grace

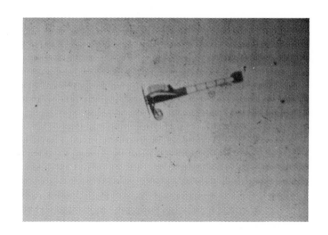

7 Drexel in a glide, August 1910

8 Drexel and Bleriot, Leopardstown 1910

Bleriots, one of which was a two-seater machine, had been damaged in transit, new timbers being fitted to the machines by a Dublin coachbuilder. The Leopardstown site was far from ideal for the weather conditions. The southwesterly winds sweeping down from the Dublin mountains hit the grandstands creating turbulence and curlover which the pilots had to contend with on both days of the meeting. High trees and fences further restricted flying. On Monday 29 August the surrounding roads were packed with motor cars, jaunting cars, ass carts and bicycles. The Dublin South East railway ran a shuttle service to Foxrock railway station. The fare was an inflated two shillings return from Harcourt Street station. By late morning the course was lined with people. Admission was two shillings and sixpence (12.5p) for the general enclosure and five shillings (25p) for the grandstand. According to the correspondent of *The Aero* magazine the whole of Dublin seemed to have turned out. The crowds did their best to avoid paying the admission charge and get a free show — even in those days! Screens had been erected along the railway embankment and a large force of Royal Irish Constabulary was present but the crowds still clambered on to roofs, climbed into trees and positioned themselves in the many fields adjoining the racecourse. Crowds were also reported on Three Rock Mountain and on Killiney Hill but they saw little and missed the excitement and atmosphere of the field itself. Seeing the machines and

9 Cecil Grace's Farman, Leopardstown 1910

pilots close up and experiencing the distinctive smell of burnt castor oil was special to those early enthusiasts. The general enclosure was one mile long and ran from the Stillorgan end of the racecourse to Foxrock railway station. The nobility and gentry who turned out in force preferred the exclusivity of the stands and the members' enclosure. The barriers were patrolled by the colourful Hussars drawn from the Cavalry depot. Their foward thinking General Lyttleton believed his men might as well get used to the aeroplanes: they would probably see them in the next war! The Band of the First Battalion Rifle Brigade provided music for the public in the general enclosure. Aviation not yet having made its mark with music composers, the public had to be content with numbers like "Ship Ahoy" and "Light Cavalry". An old lady selling apples in the general enclosure found trade a bit sluggish and hearing men calling out "Official Programmes" began shouting "Official Apples" and did a much better trade. After lunch Cecil Grace was first off flying his Farman in the strengthening breeze. He climbed to 200 ft. but had to land shortly afterwards because the metal strip securing the back of his seat broke, making it difficult for him to reach the rudder bar.

Drexel then took to the air in a single-seat Bleriot. He climbed to 400 ft. then circled the racecourse while continuing the climb to 900 ft. He landed after a ten minute flight. Dickson went next, flying his Farman biplane. After a slow take-off he just cleared the hedge and landed in the next field with engine problems. The machine was wheeled back to the hangars for inspection. Later on Drexel flew again, demonstrating turns and banking. Drexel intended to finish the demonstration with an engine-off landing but had to restart his engine to reach the field. He had misjudged the strength of the wind. Grace having effected repairs to his Farman, took to the air again and during the afternoon carried the first passenger at an air meet in Ireland.

This honour fell to Desmond Arthur from Glenomera, Co. Clare. Due to strong winds, they flew straight down the racecourse, landing at the far end. Arthur was so impressed that he went on to qualify for the Royal Aero Club certificate. At five o'clock Drexel attempted a new height record but was prevented by a rainstorm from climbing beyond 1000 ft. Dickson, in the meantime, had traced his engine trouble to the new brand of petrol. After re-fuelling, he had a quick flight in the late evening.

At the dinner held in honour of the aviators on Monday evening in the Gresham Hotel, Dublin, Moore-Brabazon and Harry Ferguson were among the 300 distinguished guests. It was the society event of the year. In the after dinner speeches, Armstrong Drexel praised the organisation at Leopardstown. Cecil Grace commented that if the Leopardstown meeting proved to be a financial success it would stand apart as the only aviation meet to do so to date in the world.

Tuesday 30 August turned out blustery with winds of over 20 mph. present for most of the day. Cecil Grace braved the elements with a flight which almost ended in disaster when a gust of wind caught the aircraft. Showing great skill he managed to land the machine without damage. He spent the rest of the day giving passengers short hops down the racecourse at a cost of £10 a head. These were the earliest of many thousands of Irish people who would first sample the delights of the aeroplane through the five minute "pleasure flight" at an air display. Dickson then decided to risk the weather and made what was to be the last flight of the meeting. His larger machine could fly better in the strong winds but he was dogged by curlover and had to land, just missing a fence by inches. Drexel, who was not well, did not fly at all on the Tuesday, but his machine was put on display. *The Aero* correspondent spotted in the crowd what must be Ireland's first genuine air display enthusiast, the forerunner of those wonderful people who are still the core of air display supporters today. "One dear old gentleman who was there on both days was evidently bent on dressing the part. Wearing a hat, his suit of clothes was almost hidden by instruments and their attendant straps. The instruments included a pair of high class binoculars, a folding Kodak of large size, an aeronoid barometer in a case, a thermos flask in a leather case and a large size telescope also in a leather case."

So ended Ireland's first aviation meeting, which had introduced the "new era" of human travel to the Irish people. The crowd was "greatly pleased by these daring aviators". It was also the first aviation meet to record a profit, £421. Sadly Cecil Grace was killed four months later when flying across the straights of Dover from France to England. He became lost in fog and crashed into the North Sea. A few weeks after the meet, Capt. Dickson was involved in the first recorded mid-air collision over Italy. He recovered from his injuries but never flew again.

By 1911, aviation had made further progress. Air races were now all the rage. England's first major air race, The Daily Mail circuit of Britain, in July 1911, was a real test of machines and pilots. The course, in stages, was over a distance of 1000 miles and offered £1,000 in prize money. The first fully successful East to West crossing from Wales to Ireland was achieved on 22 April 1912 by Englishman Denys Corbett Wilson. He flew his Bleriot monoplane from Fishguard and landed safely in a field near Enniscorthy, Co. Wexford. The flight lasted 1 hour and 40 minutes. Wilson, who had lived in Jenkinstown, Co. Kilkenny since 1909 and who had relations there, offered demonstration flights in the south east of

Ireland over the following months. On 16 May, crowds flocked to Enniscorthy to see the daring aviator in display. Special trains were laid on to cater for the event. On 10 October he gave a display at Clonmel racecourse in less than ideal conditions. The large crowd was well pleased and responded enthusiastically as he drove away after the flight. Shortly afterwards Corbett Wilson moved to France. He joined the RFC at the start of World War One and was killed when hit by anti aircraft fire on 10 May 1915.

The Aero Club of Ireland, flushed with success and funds after its first event, set about organising its first air race in 1912. The idea was to enable not only Dublin people but those all along the route to see the aircraft in flight. Starting at Leopardstown, the air race would run to Belfast and back. The date was set for 7 September. By the end of August twelve entrants were listed, competing for a prize fund of over £300. As dawn broke over the tented village at Leopardstown on race day only four competitors were left, the remainder having been scratched during the previous week for different reasons.

The first competitor was Henry Astley, flying a 70 hp. Bleriot. He was one of England's top aviators with a lot of cross country flying to his credit, including some trips to France. He took part in the Daily Mail circuit of Britain in July 1911. The next competitor was Lt. J.C. Porte RN, flying a 100 hp. Deperdussin. He was the son of the vicar of Bandon in Co. Cork. Born on 26 February 1884 he had served in the submarine section of the Royal Navy. When invalided out of the service, suffering from pulmonary tuberculosis, he took up flying. He became joint managing director of the British Deperdussin aeroplane company. The third competitor was Desmond Arthur, flying a 70 hp. Bristol. Born in Co. Clare, Arthur got his introduction to flying as the first "Irish air meet" passenger, carried by Cecil Grace. This was at the first aviation meeting in 1910 at Leopardstown. He had since learned to fly and had qualified for the Royal Aero Club certificate. Finally, there was James Valentine, flying a 50 hp. Deperdussin, the first British pilot to complete the circuit of Britain race in 1911, coming in third behind the French pilots Lt. Beaumont and Jules Vedrines. Valentine regarded his French designed Deperdussin as superior for racing to anything his fellow countrymen had yet designed.

The weather conditions were bad with gales and rain showers. Yet a huge crowd braved the elements to see the attraction. It was reported to be raining hard in Belfast. Visibility at Leopardstown was poor and Three Rock Mountain was covered in cloud. There were gusts of over 30 mph. At 2.30 pm. the French aviator, Monsieur Salmet, who was attending to do some exhibition flying, went up in his Bleriot. He flew two circuits and after much buffeting landed and reported conditions as horrible. At

10 Valentine, Salmet and Astley, Belfast 1912

11 J.C. Porte

12 Desmond Arthur

13 Deperdussin flown by Valentine, Belfast bound

4.00 pm. the weather improved slightly and Belfast was reported to be fine and sunny. The race was started, but in view of weather and failing light the organisers decided to finish the race at Belfast without a return leg.

Astley went off first, then Valentine with a spectacular take-off, jumping the hedge before climbing out over hangars, tents and crowd, which were all badly placed, not allowing a clear take-off run. There was no margin for possible engine failure. *The Aeroplane* correspondent of the day remarked that had engine failure occurred there was a choice of landing on a hangar, a tree or a petrol tent store. Arthur, flying the 70 hp. Bristol, failed to become airborne and damaged his machine when he hit a flagpole. He was forced to retire. Porte, flying the big Deperdussin rose into the air and was seen struggling to keep the craft steady in the howling wind. He flew out towards Rathfarnham then returned to land. He reported that gusts were pulling the control stick from his hands and he could never reach Belfast in such conditions. He was flying a company machine worth over £1,500. He did not wish to risk damage in an "out" landing.

Henry Astley flew as far as Newry but because of the strong headwinds had little fuel remaining. He turned back to land safely at Laytown near Drogheda. Valentine also got as far as Newry before being forced to land in a small field.

Belfast, the initial goal, was never reached and the vast crowds who had come to the Balmoral Showgrounds were bitterly disappointed. By contrast, the crowds at Leopardstown departed in happy mood, full of admiration for the pilots, having seen courageous and skilful flying in the teeth of such foul weather. The air race committee decided to divide the first prize between Astley and Valentine. Lt. Porte was awarded the "Shell" prize of £50 and Arthur received a special prize of £25. Tragically, Astley was killed two weeks later at Balmoral Showgrounds in a display organised to compensate the Belfast spectators for their air race disappointment. He was demonstrating with Valentine and Salmet above an eager crowd of 12,000 people when his engine cut out. He turned away to avoid a foced landing in the crowd and thus sacrificed flying speed. The aircraft sideslipped as a result and crashed.

Valentine remained for some time in Ireland, carrying out demonstration flights for the general public at Enniskerry, Mullingar, Cavan, Castlebar, The Curragh and Tuam.

Desmond Arthur joined the Royal Flying Corps as a Lieutenant and was killed in an accident at Montrose, Scotland on 27 May 1913. He had the dubious distinction of being one of the RFC's first casualties. Bad maintenance on the wing of his BE2 caused it to break up in mid-air.

Lt. Porte later worked on the design and improvement of flying boat technology and became known as the father of the British flying boats. After a long battle with tuberculosis he finally succumbed and died on 22 October 1919 in Brighton. During his life he was awarded many honours including the US Distinguished Service Medal for his work on the flying boat.

14 Astley's Bleriot, engine run-up

Aviation correspondents of the time were very critical of Leopardstown as a venue for aviation meetings because of obstacles and turbulent conditions. They applauded however the organisational ability of the committee and its financial success.

At the outbreak of World War One the Aero Club of Ireland was dissolved and the balance of funds raised at Leopardstown was donated to the Red Cross. The war put an end to all private flying and many young Irishmen went to serve with the Royal Flying Corps and failed to return.

Aviation in Ireland was restricted to military activities. On 1 September 1913 six biplanes of number two squadron Royal Flying Corps flew to Ireland from their base in Montrose, Scotland. They came via Stranraer and crossed the sea by the shortest route. This was the first overseas flight of the Royal Flying Corps. They participated in military manoeuvres at Rathbane Camp, Co. Limerick. In 1917 the British Admiralty established two airship bases in Ireland, one at Malahide Castle, Co. Dublin and the other at Johnstown Castle, Co. Wexford, to carry out German U-Boat patrols. Also in 1917 the Air Force established airbases at Baldonnel, Gormanstown, Collinstown, Tallaght, The Curragh, Fermoy and Oranmore. American flying boats were based at Cobh, Whiddy Island and Wexford, where the slipway built for their use can still be seen.

Two years later on 15 June 1919, Alcock and Brown landed their Vickers Vimy in a bog in Clifden, Co. Galway. It was the first west to east non-stop crossing of the Atlantic from Newfoundland, in a time of 16 hours, 28 minutes.

On Friday 8 August 1919 the RFC, which had now been renamed the Royal Air Force, held an Irish Aerial Derby. The race was to start at Tallaght aerodrome in Co. Dublin, proceed to The Curragh in Co. Kildare, Gormanstown, Co. Meath and then back to Tallaght, a distance of just over one hundred miles. The turning points were marked by large white crosses. A large crowd assembled at Tallaght for the start at five o'clock. Twenty one military machines drawn from every air base in the country took part. There was one RE8, five DH9s, four Bristol Fighters, nine Avro 504s, one SE5A and one Sopwith Camel. This assortment of aircraft was handicapped according to speed. When they had departed the field heading towards The Curragh in ideal weather conditions, the crowds at Tallaght were entertained to a flying display by Flt. Lt. Essell and Flt. Lt. Sainsbury. The racing machines meanwhile had turned at Gormanstown and were on the way back. As they flew over Dublin they came in low over the RAF HQ in Merrion Square. First past the winning post was Flt. Lt. Urmston flying a mono engined Avro 504. He completed the course in 1 hour 9 minutes and 34 seconds, an average speed of 89 mph. The *Irish Times* reported that the event was thoroughly enjoyed by all. That

The DH9. piloted by Captain Hannon, who won the Round Dublin Race, passing the Winning Post.

The two Martynside Scouts taking off in the Air Race.

Commandant Malloney and Sergeant Maher (Observer), who were second in the Race Round Dublin.

General O'Duffy congratulating one of the Free State Airmen.

.. Prenderville, who won the Landing Competition in an Avro.

Captain Hannon and his Observer (Sergeant MacNally) in the Winning Machine.

15 First Public Aerial Display by Air Corps, 1924

evening the band of 141 Squadron provided the entertainment. Shortly afterwards the Bristol F2B equipped 141 Squadron which was based at Tallaght aerodrome was moved to Castle Bromwich near Birmingham.

The Anglo Irish Treaty was signed on 6 December 1921 bringing an end to five years of insurrection in Ireland. The RAF withdrew all its units and the new Irish Free State Army took over Baldonnel in May 1922 from number two Squadron Irish Wing RAF and started to build an Air Corps. Machines were purchased in England from the .vast post-war surplus stock. Bases were opened in Limerick, Kilkenny and Waterford. The Tallaght Air Base was closed due to proximity to Baldonnel. Collinstown Air Base became Dublin Airport in 1937.

At the outbreak of civil war on 28 June 1922 the Air Corps had a total of six Bristol Fighters, four Avro 504K trainers, four Martinsyde F4 Buzzard Scouts and one SE5A Fighter. The Air Corps carried out reconnaisance patrols during this time. By the end of 1922 the Corps had fourteen pilots all of whom had flown with the RFC/RAF and most had been highly decorated. With the end of the civil war on 7 March 1924 the task of building a peacetime organisation began. A school of aeronautics was formed and the first student pilots began their training.

By 1924 the Air Corps had twenty three aircraft and twelve of these were to display for the first time to the public on the occasion of the Tailteann Games held in Dublin during the month of August 1924. Set on the style of the Olympic Games they were designed to attract Irish sportsmen from all parts of the world. Many emigrants returned for the games and the event was a great success. The Air Corps provided a flypast at the official opening of the games and this was followed by an aerobatic display. The main air display and competition took place on Friday 15 August. Twenty thousand people flocked to see their Air Service, now just two years old, displaying at the fifteen acres in the Phoenix Park, Dublin. The car parks were hard pressed. The report in *An T-Oglac*, the defence forces magazine, said it was probably the largest concentration of motor vehicles yet seen in Ireland.

The Air Corps machines were parked in front of the Chief Secretary's Lodge. Eight aircraft were to be used in the five events listed in the programme. Four were to remain in reserve. The programme opened with an exhibition of aerial drill by the eight aircraft. The display was very graceful, changing from "V" formation to Squadron formation, and was enhanced by the effect of the heavy white cumulus clouds which created a dramatic backdrop. Lt. Delamere performed an "engine out" and recovery demonstration and this section finished with a spot landing competition which was won by Lt. W. Delamere in his Avro.

The display by the pupils of the Air Corps training school had to be cancelled because of damage to one of the Avros. Capt. F.S. Crossley, Comdt. T.J. Maloney (O/C Baldonnel) and Lt. O.A. Heron flying the fast moving Martinsyde Scout, gave a thrilling display of aerobatics. Capt. Crossley performed a vertical spin, cork screwing down at terrific speed until close to the ground. Looping and rolling manoeuvres were also displayed. Lt. Heron was later to be tragically killed at another Air Corps display held in the Phoenix Park in 1933.

The next event, eagerly awaited by the crowd, was the Aerial Race. Col. C.F. Russell acted as the starter and judge. Seven machines were entered to fly around the triangular course and the Hellfire Club in the Dublin mountains was the outside turning point. The three "DeHavilland Nine" machines were allowed a three minute start and the two Bristol Fighters had a two minute start ahead of the two high powered Martinsyde Scouts which were flown by Lt. A. Russell and Lt. O. Heron. These two pilots were expected to make up the handicap and provide an exciting finish. As the first group of DH9s moved away Capt. W.I. Hannon shot ahead and was seen leading Capt. Crossley and Comdt. Maloney by half a dozen lengths. The Bristols flown by Lt. Delamere and Lt. Carrol went next, followed by the final group, the Martinsyde Scouts. The Scouts climbed high and opened up to reduce the lead. Turning at the Clondalkin Chimney mark, Lt. Russell was travelling at 145 mph. and his companion, Lt. Heron at 135 mph. Capt. Hannon in the DH9 had a commanding lead from the Hellfire Club to the Wellington monument in the Phoenix Park which was the final turning point in the race. He was followed by the other DH9s. In a last desperate effort Capt. Crossley made a daring move to cut Capt. Hannon out by swooping down to within only a few yards of the monument. He failed to gain ground and in doing so lost his position to Comdt. Maloney who got second past the flagpost, just behind Capt. Hannon. Crossley was third and Lt. Heron was fourth.

Capt. Hannon got a great ovation for his fine win. Hannon who had an excellent flying record with the RFC during the war was from Co. Limerick and before the war had been a successful amateur jockey. Obviously he never lost the racing spirit and attributed his success to the fine tuning he had given his Siddley-Puma engine. Capt. Crossley went up in the Martinsyde Scout to finish off the event with a display of trick flying befitting his reputation as a famous air ace. Some of his breathtaking manoeuvres were performed only thirty feet above the ground. The Aonac Tailteann medals were presented to the winners by Major General Eoin O'Duffy. Among the spectators that day was Lt. Blakley of the American Army Air Force who held until mid-1924 the world aerial speed record. He was astonished at the skill and resourcefulness of the Irish airmen.

On 12-13 April 1928 Comdt. J.C. Fitzmaurice of the Air Corps, together with Capt. Kohl and Baron Von Hunefeld, completed the first successful east-west non-stop crossing of the Atlantic in a heavier than air machine. They used a Junkers W33 named the Bremen. Public interest was at its height and Ireland was at the centre of aviation history in the making. Because of its geographical position Ireland was the landing and take-off point for many historic flights.

After the excitement and interest generated by the Bremen, Col. J.C. Fitzmaurice chaired a meeting of a provisional committee on 9 August 1928 at the Hibernian Hotel, Dublin. The aim was to organise a club to promote the development of civil aviation in Ireland. On the day before this meeting an Avro Avian and an Avro 504R Gosport demonstrator from A.V. Roe & Co. in England came over and gave demonstration flights to prospective club members. On the day after the meeting the two machines took fifty prospective members aloft.

The Irish Aero Club was formally inaugurated at a meeting in the Engineer's Hall, 35 Dawson Street, Dublin, on the evening of 15 August 1928. There was a large attendance and over one hundred members enrolled on that night alone. Col. Fitzmaurice presided and urged the members to do all in their power to develop civil aviation, still non-existent in Ireland. A committee was appointed which included Col. Fitzmaurice as chairman, Col. Charles Russell, Senator Oliver St. John Gogarty and Osmond Gratten Esmonde TD.

The Irish Aero Club's first machine, an Avro Avian, was purchased at a cost of £750 and registered EI-AAA on 5 October 1928, the first civil aircraft to be registered in the Irish Free State.

EI-AAA was based at Baldonnel and flying commenced on Saturday 12 January 1929. Col. Charles Russell acted as honorary instructor and fellow officers of the Air Corps generously gave of their services to train members of the club during its first year of operation. At the second AGM of the club, held at the Dolphin Hotel, Dublin on 2 February 1931, the treasurer announced a healthy surplus of £593. The government gave a grant of £1,000 to help meet the expenses of the club in developing civil aviation. To help encourage an interest in aviation and to make the public more air minded, the club decided to organise an annual air pageant. This event was to initiate the most exciting period for the development of sporting aviation in Ireland, the thirties. The era of the Barnstormers and the Flying Circus had arrived. The first pageant was held at Baldonnel on Saturday 15 August 1931. It was a great success and the public saw not only the club's own aircraft in action but also a number of visiting aircraft from the UK. An entrance fee could not be charged because Baldonnel was government property, so admission was by way of invitation tickets. The five shillings (25p) admission to the reserve enclosure included tea in the club house. The public enclosure cost two shillings and four pence (11.5p). The tax man was on the job for the four pence represented "entertainment tax", charged to any event where mechanically propelled vehicles were used. Special buses ran from O'Connell Bridge, Dublin to the aerodrome gates all day. Passenger flights were offered in the "Prince Henry", a HPW8 (Handley Page) twelve-seater airliner which the club had chartered for the day. Passengers were invited to see Dublin from the air. The HPW8 carried its passengers in great comfort, with continuous windows running the length of the cabin. It had a span of 75 ft., was 60 ft. in length and had a wing area of 1456 sq. ft. It was powered by two 360 hp. Rolls Royce Eagle VIII engines and had a range of 500 miles. This particular aircraft, G-EBBI, had entered service with Imperial Airways on 7 June 1922 on the European Routes. It was retired in March 1932.

Fifteen thousand people turned up and, even though Dublin city was enveloped in rain and mist, this rain did not extend to Baldonnel seven miles away. The bad weather insurance, the first such in Ireland, which the organisers had thoughtfully obtained was safe. High winds prevented a scheduled parachute drop but dummies were dropped instead, which most spectators took to be live parachutists. Mr. W.R. Elliott, instructor with the Aero Club and ex RAF pilot performed aerobatics as did Arthur Russell, brother of Col. Charles Russell. Flt. Lt. T. Rose in his aircraft, hotly pursued Mr. J.H. Keon in a small motor car and successfully flour bombed him, much to the delight of the crowd, many lining the roads

16 "Prince Henry", Baldonnel 1931

and fields outside the aerodrome, enjoying a free show. The winner of
the arrival competition which formed part of the display was Capt. Cazalet
from Wexford, flying a Puss Moth. All flights in the HPW8 "Prince Henry"
were booked out and there was heavy demand on the other smaller club
and air taxi machines which were available for pleasure flights. The
ordinary man and woman could at last sample at first hand the delights
and thrills of flight. Aviation for all had arrived. The Lord Mayor of Dublin,
Senator Alfie Byrne, a patron of the project, was taken for a short flight
over the Dublin mountains by club instructor Elliott. The public's education in air-mindedness was under way.

   In the summer of 1930 Hugh Cahill, a garage owner from Glasnevin,
Dublin and a member of the Irish Aero Club, travelled to London with
another Aero Club pilot and friend, J.C. Malone, to purchase a Desoutter II.
This aircraft was a three-seater monoplane. It was allocated the registration EI-AAD and became the first Irish commercial aircraft of the newly
formed Iona National air taxis and flying school. Initially based at Baldonnel the company moved in April 1931 to a rented field at Kildonan
near Finglas village, four miles from Dublin city centre. Here a hangar was
constructed and club rooms established at Ireland's first commercial airfield. By June 1931 two DH Gypsy Moth aeroplanes EI-AAF and EI-AAG
had been added to the fleet. Between August 1931 and March 1932 over
4,000 people had taken pleasure flights in these aircraft when they visited
Athy, Co. Kildare, The Curragh, Co. Kildare and Skerries, Co. Dublin.
One of the passengers Kay Malone, a sister of J.C. Malone, who lived
locally remembers looping the loop over Skerries harbour and urging the
pilot for more.

   Another company, Irish Airlines Ltd. of Waterford, gave pleasure flights
in over thirty Irish towns in the summer of 1932. It also gave aerobatic
and stunt flying displays with its Blackburn Bluebird and two Avro 504Ks.
The Bluebird came to a sticky end when it crashed at Tramore in July
1932. The pilot was uninjured.

   Also in July 1932 the Scottish flyer, twenty seven year old Jim Mollison, arrived in Ireland with his fiancee, the famous Amy Johnson, to
seek advice and to plan his attempt at the first solo crossing of the Atlantic
from east to west. He intended to take off from Portmarnock Strand,
Co. Dublin. The Irish Aero Club invited the couple to their "At Home",
held in Baldonnel on Sunday 3 July. A large crowd saw Mollison give a
thrilling exhibition of crazy flying in his Puss Moth aircraft. Jim and
Amy also gave pleasure flights to some members of the public.

   On their return to England, Mollison and Johnson were married. They
returned to Ireland on 9 August. On 18 August Jim Mollison took off
from Portmarnock Strand with 160 gallons of fuel on board. The take-

off run continued for more than one mile until finally the aircraft lifted slowly and headed west towards the Atlantic. Twenty four hours later he landed at Pennfield Ridge, New Brunswick. Another chapter in pioneering flights had been written.

On Monday 17 April 1933 the Irish Aero Club was involved in further history making when the thousands of people invited to the "At Home" in Baldonnel witnessed the first Irishman to parachute from an aircraft and land on Irish soil. This honour fell to Joseph Gilmore from Ardglass, Co. Down who was a ground engineer with the Air Corps and a member of the Irish Aero Club. He took to the air in DH60 Gypsy Moth G-ABXZ piloted by Raymond Quilter son of the manufacturer of the parachute which he used. He jumped from a height of 1800 ft. and on landing safely described the experience as "glorious". A second descent was made by Mr. James Bell, a ground engineer of the Irish Aero Club. Exhibitions of aerobatics and crazy flying were given by Club members.

Gilmore was airborne again at the Air Pageant held at the new airfield at Kildonan on Whit Monday on 5 June 1933. It was organised by Iona National Airways and 15,000 people attended. Jumping from 2500 ft.

17 Joe Gilmore, Kildonan 1933

he made a spectacular landing after side slipping past a grove of trees on the eastern side of the field to land 200 ft. from the wood.

Air Corps pilots Lts. Russell, Keane and Twohig gave a thrilling display of aerobatics in their newly delivered Avro 631 Cadets. W.R. Elliott, CFI of the Aero Club, gave a demonstration of crazy flying. Elliott also won the obstacle race the start of which was novel. The pilots stood twenty five yards away from their aircraft, put on their flying clothing, carried a glass of water to the aeroplane and finally started their engines. Pleasure flight aircraft did a brisk trade at five shillings (25p) per person for a flip.

In the Spring of 1933 Capt. J.R. King completed a survey of suitable landing fields situated close to the towns and villages around Ireland in order to accommodate the aircraft of Sir Alan Cobham's Air Circus. Sir Alan Cobham was already well known for his historic flight to Australia in 1926 for which he received a knighthood. In 1927-28 he completed a 37,000 mile circumnavigation of Africa in a Singapore flying boat. Cobham was to do more perhaps than any other pioneer to foster air-mindedness among the public in both Great Britain and Ireland between the wars. He created and organised a "Circus" of unusual and exciting aeroplanes using skilled pilots and toured cities, towns and villages bringing the good news of aviation to both the public and the politicians. Between 1932 and 1935 Cobham gave more than 1200 air displays which were seen by more than four million spectators. He carried almost one million passengers on pleasure flights.

Cobham's first of two tours of Ireland in 1933 ran from 1 to 17 July. He returned to Ireland on 12 September and ended the tour on 2 October 1933. The tour was held under the auspices of the Irish Aero Club but because it was a commercial undertaking the military base in Baldonnel was out. Hugh Cahill invited the circus to display at Kildonan aerodrome at Finglas. The circus would then tour the country together with the Irish Aero Club's training machines, Moths EI-AAI and EI-AAJ which would offer pleasure flights and trial flying lessons and hopefully enrol new members. Cobham's first display of the Irish tour took place on Sunday 2 July. The participating aircraft arrived safely at Kildonan having crossed from Scotland via Stranraer to Northern Ireland over the previous two days. On Saturday Cobham lectured on his aviation experiences to a large audience at Clerys department store in Dublin. It was the first of many lectures he would give around the country.

By Sunday morning eleven different types of aircraft had assembled on the field. Most had never been seen before in Ireland. The Cierva auto-gyro, one of the last aircraft to arrive, must have created quite a stir with its aircraft fuselage and giant rotor blades turning overhead. Piloted by

18 Sir Alan Cobham

19 Cobham Programme

A.C. Rowson, this strange craft had flown from Aldergrove, Co. Antrim where it had been attending Ulster's first civil aviation display since 1912. This had been held the previous day.

Over 14,000 people flocked to Kildonan. During the morning many took flights in the three passenger airliners, the Handley Page W10, the HP33 Clive 1 and the silver and green coloured Airspeed Ferry G-ABSI named "Youth of Ireland". In fact Cobham named all his aircraft so the public could identify with them. The Airspeed Ferry, a three engined bi-plane, which carried ten passengers had been specially designed for his touring circus to his own specifications. The main requirement was dependability, followed by good viewing from the passenger cabin, as well as short take off and landing capability. Most of the fields from which Cobham operated were rough and small. The Ferries were built in York at Airspeed Ltd. by A.H. Tiltman and Nevil Shute Norway who was to gain fame in the forties as author of such famous novels as *A Town Like Alice* and *No Highway*. G-ABSI was the prototype and a total of four were built. The Handley Page HP33 Clive 1 airliner G-ABYX "Youth of Australia" capable of carrying twenty two passengers, was powered by two 550 hp. Bristol Jupiter IX engines and built as a prototype in 1927. It was sold to Cobham in April 1933. The Handley Page W10 airliner G-EBMM "Youth of New Zealand" was built in 1925 and powered by two Napier Lion 450 hp. engines. The W10 could carry sixteen passengers and had flown with Imperial Airways on all its scheduled air routes. On retirement from airline service it was sold to Cobham's National Aviation Displays.

Other aircraft included three Avro 504Ks first built in 1919 and capable of carrying two passengers in the front seat with the dual controls removed. After the war the 504 became popular as a pleasure flight aircraft with flying establishments all over England. A DH83 Fox Moth G-ACEY "Honeymoon Express", capable of carrying four passengers in its enclosed cabin had its pilot, in time honoured fashion, braving the elements in the open cockpit. Sir Alan Cobham also displayed one of the first DH82 Tiger Moths to come off the production line. The first batch of 114 were being produced as military trainers for the RAF and other air forces. Cobham was held in such high esteem by De Havilland, having tested their prototypes and used their aircraft for many of his record breaking flights he was able to purchase the prototypes G-ABRC and G-ABUL for the circus. Nine thousand Tiger Moths had been produced by the end of 1945. Another earlier Moth, a DH60 Gypsy Moth G-ABUB, visiting Kildonan with the circus had been flown from Australia to England by Jim Mollison in July 1931. This flight created a new overland long distance record.

20 Cobham Circus 1933

21 Kildonan 1933 and (inset) learners, Junior Aviation Club

Ald. Alfie Byrne TD, Dublin's Lord Mayor, opened the show and endorsed Cobham's belief in the development of civil aviation by giving as many people as possible direct personal knowledge and experience of flying. A formation of the ten circus aircraft led by the giant HP33 Clive 1 passed over the field. This formation had flown over Dublin on Saturday to advertise the event and had brought the city to a standstill. All gazed skywards at such an unusual sight. Flt. Lt. Turner Hughes billed as the famous upside down flier and exponent of advanced aerobatics, lived up to his name in the Tiger Moth which was painted in bright yellow and fitted with an inverted fuel system for sustained flight upside down. Sir Alan Cobham gave the commentary and explained each of the manoeuvres as Hughes went through his routine. The inverted flight attracted considerable attention and Hughes flew upside down over the crowd at a height of fifty feet. Hughes had a splendid instinct for aircraft positioning to ensure maximum enjoyment by the spectators. His finish left them gasping. Rolling into normal position he climbed quickly, rolled over into inverted flight and dived at the crowd passing over at a height of about one hundred feet. They could see his upturned face, his hands on the stick and his tie fluttering in the breeze. Hughes flew with Cobham for one season only and during that time spent no less than 170 hours upside down in the Tiger. He left in the late summer of 1933 to become a test pilot for Armstrong Whitworth. Standing on top of the Avro 504, Martin Hearne demonstrated the art of wing walking. Climbing out of the cockpit while in flight he made his way out along the wing and stood arms outstretched against the bracing wires. He then climbed up to the top wing and waved to the crowd while clutching a piece of thin wire, his only life line. He would finish the act by sitting astride the skid of the 504 without a harness of any kind while the pilot performed a loop. When the aircraft landed, an invitation would go out for intrepid volunteers from the public. Later it would be announced that a volunteer had been found and Martin dressed as a farm worker would climb awkwardly into the aircraft. The pilot would take off and Martin would attempt awkwardly to climb on to the wing flipping back into the cockpit each time. Finally the pilot would bank away from the crowd and Martin would throw out a life size dummy dressed like himself. At one of the displays in Dublin an expectant mother had her baby on the spot after the shock. The act was subsequently dropped from the programme. The two parachutists Ivor Price and Miss Naomi Heron Maxwell had joined the circus as amateurs and gave daily demonstrations of the safety and life-saving attributes of the parachute. The world's first autogyro was also demonstrated. This was the Cierva two-seater autogyro designed by the Spanish inventor Don Juan de la Cierva in 1923. It was basically the fuselage of an Avro 504K without the mainplanes but fitted instead with a three bladed rotor mounted on a steel tube pylon. The rotor was not engine driven but kept in motion by the forward speed of the machine. This characteristic gave rise to the name autogyro. Fifteen of the C19 MKV were built and two flew with the circus. It was not easy to fly and did not operate well over the rough grass runways. The technique for take-off was to open the throttle while holding stationary with brakes on. When the rotor reached about 120 rpm., depending on wind strength, the starboard brake was released to allow the autogyro to swing into wind. With both brakes released and the stick well back the machine started its take-off run and rose into the air with the tail skid almost touching the ground. If the undercarriage hit a rough patch during the short take-off the machine would wobble violently in a circular motion. Among the amused ground crew this spectacle was known as the dance of death.

Once airborne first timers found it disconcerting to have rotor blades whizzing around so close to their heads. They quickly got used to this and could then concentrate on the difficult job of flying it. To land the auto-gyro the engine is throttled back and a gentle glide rate is established. The glide becomes almost vertical as the nose is held up. At about 150 ft. the nose is tilted down to generate a forward airspeed of 40 mph. At twenty feet the stick is eased back until the machine touches the ground gently.

By the end of the show the public had got their money's worth and many queued until dusk to avail of a trip in the giant red and white air-liner flown by the chief pilot of the circus Lt. H.C. Johnson. The cost of the flight was seven shillings and sixpence (38p). For the complete thrill a full aerobatic flight in the open cockpit of the Avro 504 cost £1. A short flip could be had for five shillings (25p).

Those not keen on aerobatics could ride in the three engined Airspeed Ferry flown by Capt. Joe King, whose cheery disposition put everyone at ease. Smokers were definitely out. A plaque in the cockpit proclaimed "No Smoking Allowed even for Abdullahs". Such was the popularity of pleasure flights in these machines that, given a full moon and cloudless sky, the aircraft would continue to fly passengers until all had been taken up.

At the crack of dawn on the Monday, the airfield at Kildonan was a hive of activity. The circus staff, wearing white boiler suits, were packing the equipment for travel by road to the next venue, Waterford, for an evening performance. The departure was a precision operation. Once the aircraft were on their way Sir Alan, who stayed on the field overnight in his caravan with his wife, was in the thick of it. He never seemed to stand in one spot but darted here and there directing the complex operation. Nothing escaped his eagle eye. He had the gift of inspiring people to his cause and had the respect of both his ground crew and the pilots. All worked together as a team. All were flexible and prepared to undertake any task, regardless of rank or qualification. Then the convoy of lorries and caravans, their bodywork shining with cream paint, wheels painted red, made its way to the new site. It was quite a spectacle in itself. An advance party led by Leonard Rossiter, a former press officer with the air ministry in London, had already lined up the local dignitaries. Motorcyclists had placed posters in surrounding towns and villages, inviting people to fly with Alan Cobham. Leaflets distributed in local pubs and shops carried the same message. Arrow shaped signs were attached to trees, walls and buildings pointing "To the Air Display". The venue had been selected with care, within easy reach of the town yet large enough to accommodate several thousand spectators and a stream of aircraft, including the lumbering airliners. Areas close to hills were avoided, locals would use them for a free show. The aircraft would arrive first. By the time the road convoy arrived the site was already prepared, the runway direction decided and obstacles to the flypaths efficiently removed. The land owner was amply compensated. Catering and booking tents were erected, the public address laid out and tested, enclosures roped off, tents for engineers, ground crew and officers pitched. Screens were erected which carried advertising but also hid from those not willing to pay all the fascinating activity on the field. During the afternoon a massed formation flight took place over local areas to add to the build up. By evening a steady stream of people headed for the field. The Mayor and the civic leaders had already been given flights. Support was assured.

The *Cork Examiner* ran competitions offering free flights in the airliners when the circus visited Cork. The landing field at Ballincollig just outside Cork city was attached to the military barracks there. The flying circus performed on Wednesday and Thursday 5 and 6 July. Alderman Sean French, Lord Mayor of Cork, welcomed the fliers to Ballincollig on Wednesday afternoon. Following his address the display commenced and business in Cork came to a standstill. The formation flight caused great excitement in the city. The autogyro poised almost stationary over the city centre while other craft looped and dived at church spires to the north. The giant airliner cruised over the city, its silver wings glinting in the sunlight. When the aircraft returned to Ballincollig a large crowd had assembled. It was only 23 years since the first aeroplane had been seen in Ireland so there was intense interest. Cobham addressed the crowd at the opening of the display and hoped that as a result of his visit aviation would expand at Cork. Because of its geographic position Ballincollig was unsuitable for further development so Cobham went to inspect a site at Belvelly near Little Island which had been proposed for Cork's international airport by the county surveyor Richard O'Connor. The site required the reclamation of 460 acres and was very well positioned in relation to Cork city. Unfortunately the plan did not proceed and Cork had to wait until the early sixties before it finally got an international airport.

The Cork people gave Cobham a great welcome and a large crowd turned up to listen to his talk at the Cash and Co. Department store in Patrick Street. Seven thousand attended the second day's display and there was a heavy demand for the pleasure flights. W.R. Elliott, chief flying instructor with the Irish Aero Club, flew Moth EI-AAI and generated much interest in flying lessons and the possibility of a branch in Cork. By Thursday evening the circus headed for the display site at Ballycummin Castle, four miles from Limerick city, and tragedy. After the display proper had finished on Friday evening the pleasure flight aircraft took to the air like flies. There were at least eight aircraft in the circuit. In his book, *A Time to Fly*, Cobham refers to the incident as follows. "Geoffry Tyson was flying the Fox Moth with four passengers on board and suddenly found himself without an undercarriage so that he had to make a belly landing. He did this most delicately in soft grass and his passengers were unhurt and even unaware that anything unusual was happening. It wasn't his fault. A local Irish pilot had insisted on joining in with the display aircraft without bothering with the necessary discipline. He had flown beneath Geoffrey's aircraft and had wiped off the undercarriage. He and his passenger were both killed". The Irish pilot involved was William Elliott CFI of the Irish Aero Club. He was flying the Club's Moth. Visibility was bad as the sun was low in the sky. The passenger who was on his first flight was William Ower a motor mechanic from Newcastle West. That night the police advised the circus members to keep a low profile. They were also advised not to leave the field.

As dusk approached hundreds of irate and threatening people surrounded the field carrying burning torches. The local gardai ensured that it did not get out of hand: no one slept at the camp that night. Despite the tragedy, business was not affected and endless queues formed as the tour continued around the country. The tour gave its last display in Dundalk on Sunday 16 July before departing for England without further incident. The *Daily Express* proclaimed that "all Ireland seems to be taking to the air this Summer with many aerial pageants being held including the Cobham's Circus tours." Cobham's circus performed at over three hundred locations in the British Isles in that one year of 1933.

Midland and Scottish Air Ferries Ltd. who had inaugurated a scheduled service to the Isle of Man from Speke and Liverpool using its Airspeed Ferries and Fox Moths, was keen to expand its activities into Ireland. To promote the proposed service from Cork to Dublin to Liverpool, it organised displays in the two Irish cities. The first display was held in Dublin on Saturday 5 August in conjunction with the Irish Aero Club. It was to be dogged with tragedy. The first accident occurred on the Thursday evening before the show when during a rehearsal of the formation flying Lt. Jim Twohig who had been a pilot with the Air Corps since 1926 was killed. His Avro Cadet collided with another Air Corps machine during a turning manoeuvre and spun from 700 ft. to the ground.

A crowd of 30,000 assembled at the fifteen acres in the Phoenix Park, Dublin to see the Minister for Industry and Commerce Sean Lemass open the display. A fleet of twelve visiting machines took part as well as aircraft from the Air Corps and the Aero Club. Pleasure flights were given by Midland and Scottish Air Ferries using their two Airspeed Ferry aircraft G-ACBT and G-ACFB and a three engined high wing transport, the Avro 618/10 G-ACGF, which carried eight passengers and two crew and was normally used on their internal services.

Four Fox Moths, an Avro Cadet and Tutor aircraft, together with two Dragons similar to the aircraft to be used by Aer Lingus on its inaugural flight three years later, provided the flying displays. The all metal constructed Ford Trimotor G-ACAE which could carry fourteen passengers was on a visit from the Ford motor works at Dagenham. Sean Lemass had a flight in this machine during the display. G-ACAE had been purchased by the Guinness family to commute between their private airfield in Chapelizod, Co. Dublin to London and to other business capitals in Europe. Joe Gilmore made another of his now famous parachute drops. An international relay had teams representing Ireland, Scotland and England. Each team of three pilots had one aircraft. The first pilot flew one circuit of a triangular course and landed between two lines marked out on the field to hand the aircraft over to the next member of the team. Among the pilots on the Scottish team was nineteen year old Winfred Drinkwater, the youngest holder of the B licence in the British Isles. The race was hard fought but Ireland emerged victorious represented by three Air Corps pilots Lt. Arthur Russell, Lt. F. O'Cathain and Lt. T.J. Hanley who was to join Aer Lingus in 1938 and become the first of a long line of Air Corps pilots to continue with a career in Irish civil aviation. This was the first aerial pageant in which the Air Corps had a large input. They presented three different items including an air drill in which three aircraft flown by corps flying instructors were tied together with light material which would break on the slightest loss of position. Formation flight with Avro Cadet aircraft and a demonstration of an anti-aircraft battery in action completed the display.

Tragedy struck again during the air combat sequence when three fighter aircraft launched a mock attack on a two-seater Vickers Vespa

22 Air Corps Vickers Vespa. Type that crashed

single engined observation aircraft. The pilot of the Vespa Capt. Oscar Heron, an Armagh born British fighter ace who served with the RFC in World War One, and his observer Pte. Richard Tobin from Rosslare entered a spin at fifty feet and crashed to the ground. A group of doctors including Dr. Oliver St. John Gogarty and Dr. S.V. Furlong rushed to the crash scene but Capt. Heron died on his way to the military hospital in the Park. Pte. Tobin died later from his injuries. Heron had attained the rank of Major and had become a squadron leader in the RFC. During the war he had shot down eighteen German planes in combat and had won several distinctions. He had joined the Irish Air Corps at its inception. His French-born wife who was watching the display witnessed the tragedy. The display continued and the public address proclaimed that Heron had been severely injured with Tobin sustaining less severe injuries.

Because of the tragedy the Air Corps withdrew from the Cork air carnival over the next two days at Ballincollig. On Sunday afternoon the formation of Midland and Scottish Air Ferries and Irish Aero Club aircraft passed over the city. The August bank holiday weekend was fine and a large crowd turned out. Many of them took pleasure flights over the lakes of Killarney. The flying programme once again consisted of aerobatics, formation flight and crazy flying. Joe Gilmore gave his first parachute demonstration for the Cork crowds. He had been jumping now for four months and had some hair raising incidents. Because of this Joe swore by the religious medal borrowed from Johnny Maher, a buddy in the Air Corps, who later became Aer Lingus's first engineer, complete with the now famous biscuit tin of spares. The medal had a history of cures and Joe never made a parachute jump without it. Gilmore was now concentrating more on flying and had built his own aircraft in which he was to put up more than 300 hrs. He left the Air Corps in 1935 where he was employed as a civilian mechanic and joined BOAC where he worked on the Mayo composite flying boats. He was killed in an air crash in Canada in 1945.

Midland and Scottish commenced the first commercial passenger service between Liverpool and Baldonnel on Monday 14 August 1933. This ceased however on 30 September because of poor passenger numbers and a government requirement that they form an Irish company. The company itself ceased operations in 1934.

Sir Alan Cobham returned for his second tour of Ireland on 12 September 1933. He gave his first display at Carlow. The only display in the Dublin area was at Portmarnock on Sunday 17 September when thousands flocked to see the performances. Martin Hearne, the wing walker, disclosed while in Sligo that he had some association with the area. His cousin had married local doctor W.I. Cowell and now lived in Dublin. Hearne's own parents were of Irish descent. Just as the circus was to leave Ireland on Sunday 1 October a Spartan single engined mono plane owned by Aerofilms crashed at Colpe farm near Drogheda. It was piloted by thirty five year old Capt. K. Rose a photographer with Aerofilms and a former pilot in the Canadian Air Force. Rose was not one of Cobham's display pilots but was attached to the circus giving pleasure flights. The plane stalled just after take off killing Rose and injuring Mr. Patrick Hoe and his wife. Thankfully Mr. and Mrs. Hoe made a complete recovery.

In comparison to the hectic summer of 1933 display activity in 1934 was very quiet. The Cork Aero Club which had been formed as a branch of the Irish Aero Club held a display to mark the opening of their club at the Air Corps field at Fermoy on 24 June 1934. The president was Richard O'Connor who had worked so hard to get a proper airport for Cork. The weather on the day was not good and the Dublin aircraft could not get in. Local Air Corps pilots based at Fermoy, Lt. Keane and Lt. Hanley, saved the day with a fine display of stunt flying. Irish Aviation Day, planned by the Irish Aero Club to take place in August 1934, was cancelled due to a newspaper strike.

On Sunday 12 May 1935 the National Aviation Day organised by the Irish Aero Club in co-operation with the Army Air Corps and Sir Alan Cobham's Circus was held in good weather in the Phoenix Park. It was the largest display held in the country and incorporated Cobham's tour of Ireland which had started on Friday 3 May at Carlow. The circus still featured its main attractions, the daring wing walking of Martin Hearne, the two parachutists and the autogyro which had been dubbed the "Windmill Plane" by the newspapers. Geoffry Tyson who had been pilot of the pleasure flight Fox Moth was elevated to the status of star aerobatic pilot following the departure of Turner Hughes. Tyson had undoubtedly a head for inverted flight and on 25 July 1934 to commemorate the twenty-fifth anniversary of Louis Bleriot's crossing of the English Channel had flown the circus Tiger Moth G-ACEZ inverted from the English to the French coastline. He was suspended upside down held in by his seat harness for twenty minutes. On another occasion Tyson had a very close escape from disaster while suspended in the inverted position. He was flying at 600 ft. when the pin holding his safety harness came out. The Tiger went into a dive. Tyson held on to the stick with one hand and grabbed the instrument panel with the other. Keeping cool he recovered from the dive at tree top level.

The Tiger had a nine inch arm, with a hook attached, positioned on the bottom wing to allow the Tiger to perform yet another stunt. With the aid of the hook Tyson picked up a handkerchief from the ground. He

23 Geoffry Tyson picks up hankey with wing tip

did this successfully at over 800 displays. It was a superb demonstration of both Tyson's ability and the Tiger's controlability. He lived to the ripe old age of seventy nine and died in July 1987.

Another novel demonstration at the Irish displays in 1935 was the silence and beauty of glider flight. At the Dublin display there were three different glider demonstrations. Mrs. Joan Meakin had established a long distance record for women in England with a flight of fifty two miles. This plucky redhead christened the "Glider Girl" demonstrated her high performance German Wolf glider. It was fitted with a radio which enabled her to talk through the manoeuvres over the public address as she carried them out. The Ulster gliding club gave a display of loops and stalls while members of the Dublin and Baldonnel gliding clubs demonstrated how a novice learns to fly on primary gliders. Gliding in Ireland was still in its infancy. The Dublin Gliding Club had been formed in March 1934 and had purchased its first glider from the Ulster Gliding Club. It was now building a second glider at Baldonnel with the assistance of the Air Corps who had started its own club. In September 1934 the Irish Gliding Association was formed to cater for the growing number of clubs and its first president was the Minister for Defence Mr. Frank Aiken.

The now familiar formation of Cobham's aircraft led by the twenty two seater airliner arrived at the Phoenix Park just after noon on Sunday 12 May 1935 having given a display at Leopardstown the day before. This was a nostalgic return to the site which had hosted Ireland's first display twenty five years earlier. There was great activity on the ground below in the fifteen acres, a vast open green area within the park now transformed into a huge aerodrome with enclosures set out for the crowds and their cars. Catering facilities, tents and stands, were in position. Wind socks and flags moved gently in the light breeze. Officials and army officers were hurrying about dealing with last minute details as the strains of the Garda Band drifted across the field. The crowd of over 60,000 was assembling to select the best vantage points and to join the queues for the pleasure flights. Over 400 boy scouts in their smart uniforms were there to marshal the enclosures.

The display commenced with the arrival of the fourteen aircraft which had been entered in the international air rally. Two Caudron Fregate monoplanes flown by pilots of the French Air Force were the first to arrive. The winner was Miss Hallinan, a member of the Cork Aero Club. Fl. Lt. Rose from London came second. Sean O h-Uaidhaigh, president of the Irish Aero Club, a tireless worker for the cause of aviation in Ireland, introduced Sean Lemass, the Minister for Industry and Commerce. Lemass in his speech looked forward to regular air services to and from Ireland in the near future.

24 Parachute pull-off technique

The Air Corps and the Army provided the highlight of the four and a half hour display with an anti-aircraft defence and aerial attack sequence, which opened with the sound of an air raid siren. With much smoke and flashes the battle began. The AA batteries defended the field while the aircraft arrived and bombed a magazine located in the middle of the airfield. This finally exploded with a thunderous report and the victorious Avros Nos. 10, 11 and 12 and Vespas Nos. 5 and 7 returned to base, mission accomplished.

Two Cobham parachutists demonstrated the pull-off technique by deploying their chutes while standing on the wings of the airliner. Joe Gilmore gave his last parachute demonstration in Ireland. He was shortly to leave for England.

The total gate for the day was £2,966. The admission fee per car was ten shillings (50p) to the reserved enclosure. It was five shillings for the unreserved enclosure and pedestrians got in for one shilling. Having paid expenses and the entertainment tax of £566 the Irish Aero Club had a profit of £1,594. It was splendid entertainment and a triumph of organisation.

The 1935 display tour continued and on the following weekend arrived in Cork. This was to be the first display at Cork's new airfield at Farmer's Cross, opened in September 1934. It was located four miles from the city centre on the Kinsale road and was the new base for the Cork Aero Club. Ten aircraft from the circus as well as the Irish Aero Club touring machine landed at Farmer's Cross. Much interest was shown in Miss Meakin's gliding display, the first such act seen in Cork. She was towed aloft by the Avro to a height of 3,000 ft. at which point she released the cable and began her graceful display aerobatics. Three Avro Tutors carried out formation flight tied together with streamers, looping and diving as one machine.

Rain and low cloud caused the cancellation of the display due at the old military landing field at Oranmore, Galway on 21 May. Some of the disappointed crowd hired special buses to take them sixty miles north to Castlebar to see the next day's display. It was market day in Castlebar. Farmers who had made successful cattle sales arrived at the display in good spirits. One bought up all the seats in the twenty two seat airliner so he could take an aerial drive, as he called it, over his own farm. The final display of the tour was given in perfect weather on 24 May at Clooncoose Racecourse, Longford and by evening the crews were heading back for a display at Liverpool.

Seven days later, as the circus was performing at Woodford in Cheshire, Ivor Price the star parachutist was killed. He had made many hundreds of jumps during the course of his displays with Cobham. The cause of the accident was tragically simple. Ivor, while packing his chute, had forgotten to remove the handkerchief he used to hold the parachute shroud lines together as he folded the parachute into its pack. At 2,000 ft. Price jumped in formation with Miss Heron Maxwell as usual. As was his habit he delayed opening the chute until he reached a height of 1,000 ft. When he pulled the cord the parachute came out of the bag and trailed above him unopened. He was killed instantly.

Remarkably the circus carried a million passengers over the four years of its operation. It did have a number of non-fatal crashes and a good many close shaves but considering the state of the art in those days and the improvised conditions under which they were operating, the incidents were few in number. At the end of 1935 Cobham sold the display to C.W.A. Scott who together with Tom Campbell had achieved fame as the winners of the England to Australia race in 1934. Cobham could see that the heroic age of the circus was coming to an end. Commercial air transport was becoming a reality and the missionary could now safely retire from his work. There were other areas to be explored. Cobham now wanted to concentrate on the development of in-flight re-fuelling techniques. He

invented a method which he was to perfect and which is widely used today. His son Michael is the present manager of the company Flight Refuel-
ling Ltd. Sir Alan Cobham KBE, AFC died in October 1973 at the age of
seventy nine.

Scott's circus which was on a much smaller scale than Cobham's, came
to Ireland in May 1936 and commenced with a display in the Phoenix
Park on Sunday 10th. The event was once again run under the auspices
of the Irish Aero Club. Two Airspeed Ferries were the main aircraft used
for pleasure flights. A Tiger Moth and three Avro Cadets performed aerobatic and formation stunt flying. The Avro 504 was used for Martin Hearne
who was still performing his wing walking act without a parachute or
safety harness and continued to lead a charmed life. Joan Meakin featured
her gliding display accompanied by a Douglas Drone powered glider flown
by Martin Hearne. Idwal Jones replaced Tyson as the man who picked up
the handkerchief and provided many other aerobatic manoeuvres. Also
on show was the Flying Flea G-AEFK, then taking the flying world by
storm. Designed by Frenchman Henri Mignet it was an aircraft which
could be built at home for a total cost of £100. Many kits were purchased

25 The Flying Flea, Scott's Circus 1936

by enthusiastic would-be aviators until the Air League in England tested one of the machines in a wind tunnel and found the design aerodynamically unsound. This explained the nasty accidents which had been happenning to the type. The Flying Flea or Pou de Ciel was banned at the end of 1936 and all existing machines grounded.

American parachutist A.L. Harris dropped from 2,000 ft. and fell in freefall for a few seconds. One of England's first female aerobatic pilots Mrs. Winifred Crossley showed the crowd what the fair sex was capable of. She had been flying for three years and had been introduced to the sport by a pleasure flight with Cobham's circus. Scott's tour ended on 18 June 1936 and the last display before returning to England was given at Leopardstown racecourse.

Scott's flying circus wound up in early 1937 and he resumed air racing. The final display organised by the Irish Aero Club before the war was to open a fifty day tour by Aircraft Demonstrations. This display was to tour in Summer 1937 in conjunction with the Irish Aero Club's Moth EI-AAU, flown by club CFI StJohn Kearney. The Aircraft Demonstrations display was very small in comparison to previous years and only ten thousand turned out on Sunday 30 May to witness the event at Phoenix Park. Birdman Harry Ward gave the first and only demonstration of the true Batman in action when he dropped from an aircraft just two miles above the Park. He stretched out his arms with strapped canvas wings attached and swooped across the sky giving all the appearance of a giant bat in flight. Folding his wings he then deployed his parachute and made a normal landing despite strong winds. His act had a high element of danger. American Clem Sohn who developed the stunt had been booked to display at Dublin but was killed on 25 April while displaying in France. Scotsman Jock Bonar spun, looped and flicked his Avro Cadet and Capt. Rimmer gave a display of gliding. Ireland's national airline Aer Lingus, which was formed in 1936 with Sean O hUadhaigh as its first chairman displayed its two aircraft the DH Dragon "Iolar" and the DH86 named "Eire" and attracted much interest on static display.

A large crowd attended the display given in Cork on Sunday 10 July. Many people took the opportunity to fly in the Airspeed Ferry which was being sponsored for the tour by *Irish Press* newspapers.

In September 1937, the Irish Aero Club was involved in organising the King's Cup Air Race, an annual race held around Britain. This was the first time there was a stop in Southern Ireland. The twenty one competitors were hosted royally at the Dublin night stop. The IAC was praised for its efforts. After the event the bills came, mostly from the Dept. of Defence as the Air Corps had been contracted by the club to provide transport and other services including maintenance of the competing aircraft. This moved an already delicate financial situation very much into the red. After much agonising the council decided it could not trade out of the situation and wound up the IAC at the end of 1937. This was a sad end to an organisation very much to the fore in the golden era of Irish aviation and during the barnstorming air circus years from 1928 to 1938. It had provided many thrills for the Irish public and provided flying lessons at reasonable cost for student pilots.

With the outbreak of war in 1939 neutral Ireland grounded all private aircraft. Each aircraft was disabled by the authorities who removed some vital part to ensure that the owner would not be tempted to fly. All airfields and landing strips not in military hands were staked with railway sleepers. Private aviation went into hibernation and was sustained for the time being by aeromodelling activities and lectures run by the Junior Aviation Club.

26 Cobham Display Autogyro, Phoenix Park 1935

27 Cobham Circus over Co Cork, 1935 Tour

2
A Host of Venues

*28 Hydrogen Balloon being inflated,
Weston 1956*

The Irish Aviation Club was formed in April 1946 to represent all aspects of sport aviation in Ireland. It became affiliated to the Federation Aeronautique Internationale in September of the same year. The president was Sean O hUadhaigh. Chris Bruton was secretary and Denis Greene was treasurer. Following the austerity and misery of the war years the next significant air displays in Ireland had to wait until the Aero Club of Ireland was formed in 1954. This Club was renamed The Leinster Aero Club shortly afterwards to avoid confusion with the existing Irish Aviation Club. The Chief Flying Instructor of the Aero Club of Ireland was Capt. Darby Kennedy, a captain with Aer Lingus. He was supported by founder member George Donoghue and the first Hon. Secretary, David Montgomery. They set about organising their first display, held on the Whit weekend 29 and 30 May 1955. They were to set a new standard in post war air displays, encouraging aviation in all its forms. Some 50,000 people were reported to have attended the first day of the show. It was Aer Lingus's nineteenth birthday and the airline was celebrating more than two million passengers carried. Appropriately, Aer Lingus opened the show with the new Viscount series 707 which had been delivered to Dublin the year before. Flown by chief pilot Capt. R.B. Seigne, EI-AGI made a low level flypast and then demonstrated flight with just two of the four engines operating.

Capt. Darby Kennedy on whose airfield the display was held, gave a thrilling display of aerobatics. Capt. Kennedy had served as first officer with Imperial Airways, London, before joining Aer Lingus where he was their chief pilot from 1945 to 1947. He had learned to fly at Baldonnel in 1931. He had been actively engaged in promoting public interest in sporting flying in Ireland since 1938 and had taught hundreds of pilots to fly at Weston. One of his pupils, his daughter Rosemary, aged nineteen, demonstrated the skills she had learned when she spun her aircraft twenty turns from a height of 4,000 ft. down to 1,000 ft. Her proud father provided a running commentary.

51

The Dublin Gliding Club was re-constituted in 1952 having been interrupted like other aviation sports because of the war. It operated from Weston until it moved to the military airfield at Baldonnel at the end of 1955. Club pilots Sean O'Brien, John Byrne, Ken Mellor and Freddy Heinzl, a former member of the Luftwaffe, demonstrated loops and fly pasts in their gliders. Freddy became an adopted Irishman in a fascinating way. He was flying a Heinkel bomber engaged in attacking shipping coming out of Liverpool. Hit by flak the bomber limped down the Irish Sea. Freddy realised they would not make their home base in Northern France so he headed for the south coast of neutral Ireland and crash landed on a beach in Wexford. Alighting from the damaged aeroplane the crew were unsure how to use the flare which was designed to destroy the aircraft, the code books and the maps. They asked a local member of the gardai who had arrived on the scene for a match and promptly tried to set fire to the fuel in the tanks of the Heinkel. This was unsuccessful so they resorted to raking the aircraft with the machine guns they had removed from the aircraft. This worked well and the Heinkel was destroyed. Freddy spent the rest of the war in the Curragh. He thought Ireland a comical place and fell in love with its ways. He married a local girl and set up business here after the war. He was one of the founder members of the Dublin Gliding Club (1952) having been a glider pilot in Germany before the war.

The Air Corps then appeared over Weston flying Spitfires and Chipmunks which zoomed over the crowds at tree top level in perfect wingtip-to-wingtip formation. The skills of parachuting were demonstrated by French army jumper Lt. Julian Bongeot, a veteran of Indo-China and Tunisia. He made a jump from 12,000 ft., opening his parachute at 1,000. A low level drop was made by English parachutist P.K. Rayner. A flour bomb attack on "Fort Donohue" by four club Tiger Moths ended the show in a light vein.

At the conclusion of the display the Shell silver rosebowl trophy was presented to David Montgomery by the Irish Aviation Club for his work in encouraging sport aviation in Ireland. He had been the hard working secretary of the Aero Club. Sadly he was killed in an air crash the following year when his Tiger Moth crashed near Weston in September 1956.

Weston's second annual air display was again held over the Whit weekend 20 and 21 May 1956 and was opened by the then Tanaiste, William Norton, who congratulated the club on creating a deeper interest in aviation in Ireland. Billed as Ireland's biggest yet air display it demonstrated many firsts before a crowd of over 50,000 people. The Gloster Meteor Jet WA 634 was sent by the Martin Baker Company, manufacturers of ejection seats, to demonstrate a low level ejection first carried out successfully less than a year earlier on 3 September 1955. On that day Sqd. Ldr. John Fifield had safely ejected from this aircraft at a speed of 120 mph. along Chalgrove runway in Oxford. The seat ignited correctly and he was shot clear of the Meteor to a height of seventy feet. The parachute fully deployed at thirty feet, to allow a safe descent. At Weston a dummy was ejected with a thunderous bang from the Meteor, flown by Capt. J.E.D. Scott. It shot high into the air, the parachute deployed and it landed safely at the far end of the field. The jet returned to Dublin airport. This jet, the first one to appear at an Irish display, is today preserved in the Aerospace Museum at RAF Cosford, West Midlands.

James Martin, chief designer and founder of the Martin Baker Aircraft Co. was an Ulsterman born in Crossgar, Co. Down. The many different types of ejection seats he designed had by 1980 saved 4,700 lives and this number grows steadily every year.

The first balloon to be flown in Ireland since the beginning of the century made its appearance when Dutch husband and wife balloonists, Dr. Jo and Nina Boesman, displayed the Balloon Club of Holland's gas balloon PH-BLI on tether. The weather was far from suitable with blustery conditions but they managed to fly it up to a height of 100 ft. A polished fifteen minute performance was provided by the Air Corps who were flying three Spitfire two seat trainers in a "V" section flypast, followed by a Provost trainer which made low level aerobatics look almost easy. Rene Vincent, a plumber from Paris, stunned the crowd with a triple parachute descent from a height of 2,500 ft. He was one of the first licensed parachutists in France and the creator of this stunt which he had performed more than 450 times. The first chute was attached to the jump aeroplane. Vincent cut from this. The second chute then deployed. This chute in turn was cut away and he descended under the third parachute. All this for a modest fee of £60 for the performance.

At this display Leitrim born Freddy Bond was to make history by becoming the first Irishman to make a sport parachute drop in Ireland. Freddy at the tender age of fourteen had watched the Cobham parachute displays in Longford and decided to become a parachutist. During the war he was a British Army paratrooper. He wished to see the sport developed in Ireland. With moral support provided by Rene Vincent, Freddy made his first jump from the Dragon flown by Capt. Darby Kennedy. In free-fall he had problems with his ripcord and had to tug with both hands before the rip pulled and released the canopy. Sailing over the crowd he hit the ground with such a thump that his helmet smashed. Undaunted Freddy later went to England for a course on parachute inspection and packing and on his return he founded the Irish Parachute Club and became its first chief instructor.

30 Gloster Meteor

*29 Freddie Bond, Ireland's first
sport parachutist*

There was much to entertain the crowds on the ground as well, with the Aer Rianta educational section providing a static display of historical models. The Air Corps put Seafire F3 no. 157 on display for the public to climb over. Aer Lingus showed a working model of the Dart turbo-prop engine that powered the Viscount, a plane which had displayed for the crowds earlier in the day. A light relief act almost backfired when a feigned attempt to steal a parked aircraft proved too realistic for some of the crowd. Women grabbed children and many people rushed away from the barrier in panic – the realism of the snatch was overwhelming.

Among the visiting airmen was air ace Group Captain Douglas Bader who had such a distinguished career in World War Two and became an inspiration to the handicapped by overcoming a double leg amputation. Having been fitted with artificial limbs he resumed flying with the RAF and played a major role in the Battle of Britain. He flew into Weston in his privately owned Gemini aircraft.

The first large display to be held in the Limerick area after the war took place on Sunday 26 May 1957 when the Shannon Aero Club organised a display at Shannon Airport. It was held in conjunction with "An Tostal",

31 Bond preparing for drop from Tiger Moth, Weston

32 Air Corps Seafire No 157 on static display, Weston 1957

a Spring festival promoted by Bord Failte, the Irish Tourist Board, to encourage tourism. It was called "An Tostal Air Show". Bord Failte agreed to underwrite the financial risk up to £1,250. Happily the club did not need to call on this: the display was held in glorious sunshine. Two thousand two hundred cars and 13,000 spectators were checked through the gates. A further 2,000 spectators evaded the net and got in free of charge. Bogus collectors one mile down the road also made a quick killing. Long queues of cars were reported at the peak time just after lunch, with tail backs to Ennis and Bunratty and a slow crawl on the single road to the airport. The hot sun beamed down and thousands baked in their cars in the slow moving traffic. Cars of that era were painted in the utility black colour and having no sun roofs many tempers frayed. Two car engines overheated and were burned out. Passengers on the CIE shuttle buses fared no better. Those who survived the trip were treated to a first class display. Sean Lemass, the Minister for Industry and Commerce, opened the show. The Mayor of Limerick, G.E. Russell, in his introduction said it was due to Lemass's courage and foresight that Shannon had developed to its present dimensions. "A few years ago the area in which the airport has been built was wasteland. We have now what has been truly called the crossroads of the world."

The show was opened by the Irish Air Corps proudly displaying two of their Vampire jets for the first time. They were the first jets to join the Air Corps fleet and had been delivered in July 1956. A formation of Air Corps piston engined Provosts also gave a display. Aer Lingus demonstrated the Vickers Viscount 707 EI-AGI "St. Laurence O'Toole". The company was celebrating its twenty first year serving the Irish public. The 707 went on static display for the public before returning to Dublin three hours later to resume scheduled services. Ranald Porteus demonstrated the Auster J/5L Aiglet's exceptional handling qualities, a reason for its increasing popularity as an ideal club aircraft for both training and aerobatic flight. It was suitable for trick flying and could touch down on one wheel with a high degree of control. One of the highlights was Frenchman M. Rene Vincent who had astounded crowds at Weston the year before. After take off in the Tiger Moth he threw out a rope ladder and, climbing to the bottom rung, he suspended himself with one hand and then one foot. At 1500 ft. he jumped from the trapeze and landed by parachute. This act was considered so dangerous by the French authorities that it had been banned. Rene Vincent more than earned his fee of £120 plus air fare. Later on in the show he did a triple parachute descent. Not to be outdone, parachutists Freddy Bond and Norman Hoffman of Dublin and Vic Williams from Mullingar made a triple parachute drop. They carried Irish flags while descending and created a beautiful spectacle against the clear blue sky. Local fliers led by Chris Humfreys, an ex RAF pilot, performed formation flights using Tiger Moths and club member Sam Pratt displayed the Chipmunk. A scheduled flight, a TWA DC4 which flew in from Frankfurt added to the international flavour, as did Seaboard and Western who put their Curtis C46 Commando aircraft no. N10427 on static display for the afternoon. Capt. Darby Kennedy of Weston provided pleasure flights in his Dragon. A gliding display was given by the members of the Limerick and Dublin gliding clubs and control line flying was demonstrated by the local aeromodellers. In a letter to the hard working display organiser Paddy Duggan of the Shannon Aero Club, Martin McGuire owner of the Curraghgower mills in Limerick praised the voluntary effort of such an extensive operation and the fact that they had overcome all the difficulties and frustrations in this the first event to be held at Shannon. "I am always impressed when men subordinate their personal feelings for a common cause and can be relied upon to carry out the task allotted to them, be it complicated or simple."

Shannon Aero Club set high standards for their first show and gained valuable experience. Hopes of building this show into an annual international air pageant were dashed when the then Department of External Affairs refused foreign military participation, including promised USAF aircraft. Today we live in more enlightened times. Just two weeks later the third annual air display was held at Weston over the Whit weekend. The dedicated committee for the 1957 show was headed by Capt. Darby Kennedy, George Donoghue and the Hon. Secretary Ernest Verso. This team had successfully established the event in the public's mind as one of Ireland's main Whitsun attractions. The show was opened by Patrick Lynch chairman of Aer Lingus and Aer Rianta. In his opening address he remarked on the progress the club had made in training civilian pilots. "Surely there was no industry to which pioneers and amateurs had contributed more than to civil aviation".

The young lady on her flying trapeze proved a most novel attraction when thirty three year old Parisian circus woman Mlle Andree Jan suspended from a Bell 47 helicopter, hovered one hundred feet above the ground. She performed many circus acrobatic routines with the ropes but without the benefit of the safety net. Then to prove the point she hung from the trapeze first with her teeth and then with her feet as the helicopter circled the enclosure. This had been her five hundred and fifth time to perform the act. The Air Corps flew three Spitfires in formation flight. Sadly this was to be the last performance of both the Spitfire and the Seafire, the naval version with the capability of folding its wings. Only twenty Spitfire T9 two seat conversions were made and the Air Corps bought six of them, numbers 158 to 163. The first machines were delivered

in 1951. The Air Corps operated twelve Seafires (146-157) delivered in
1947. At the end of their service life these aircraft were scrapped and Seafire 157 was transferred to Bolton Street College of Technology, Dublin
to be used as an instructional airframe. The Spitfires were sold to the UK
in the early 1960s and took part in the Battle of Britain film in 1968.
One of the Air Corps Spitfires had in fact been credited with one ME 109
victory while flown by a French pilot in the real Battle of Britain. When
the film was completed the aircraft were dispersed. Two went to museums
in the USA and number 162 was fully restored by Nick Grace and made
a nostalgic return to Baldonnel at Air Spectacular '86. Sadly none were
retained in Ireland. The Department of Defence had offered three Spitfires for sale at £1,500 each but despite efforts to keep one example for
restoration in Ireland all went abroad. The 1988 value of a fully restored
Spitfire is in excess of £300,000.

After the Seafire display the Air Corps unveiled for the first time to
the Weston crowds two of their three Vampire jets (numbers 185, 186
and 187) which had been delivered to the service late the previous year.
They screamed low across the field before showing off their impressive
climbing power. The pilots were Capts. Liddy and Whelan. Joss Yates,
the representative in Ireland for Westland Aircraft, introduced the Westland Widgeon, a five seat general purpose helicopter. No helicopters were
yet operated in Ireland either by the military or by commercial interests.
The Widgeon demonstrated its capability for air/sea rescue work. Joss
was well aware of the value of helicopters in rescue work abroad and their
many potential uses in Ireland. For the next five years Joss pressed for
the use of the rescue helicopter in Ireland. His efforts fell on deaf ears it
would appear. The Air Corps finally took delivery of their first helicopter
for air/sea rescue in November 1963.

Parachutists led by Freddy Bond, Vic Williams and Norman Hoffman
were joined by Welshman Brian Johnston to attempt the first mass parachute drop in the British Isles and Ireland. To make it even more dramatic
for the public they used three jump aircraft. Freddy brought up the rear
in a Tiger Moth flown by his good friend Capt. "Monkey" Morgan who
would have no truck with this parachuting nonsense and could not understand why sane people would jump out of a perfectly serviceable aircraft.
Finally Freddy's moment arrived and seeing the others jump safely he
launched himself. When he deployed his parachute he realised he was so
far behind the group that he would not make the field and was heading
instead straight for a gypsy camp site. He came in with a crash beside an
old lady bedecked in a shawl who was crouched over her campfire. Pots
and pans scattered in all directions and when the uproar had settled,
Freddy dusted himself down and enquired whether there was any tea in

33 Andree Jan suspended from Bell Helicopter, Weston 1957

34 Westland Widgeon, Weston 1957

the pot. The old lady who had not seen him coming agreed to join him in a cup to settle her shattered nerves!

Demonstrations of control line Model Aircraft were mounted by members of MACI (Model Aircraft Council of Ireland). The Dublin Gliding Club pilot John Byrne was towed aloft in his glider to begin a cross country flight. After travelling twenty miles he landed in Dunlavin. Also on display at the show was Piper Apache EI-AJL a twin engined four seater which was the first Irish registered light aircraft to cross the Atlantic. This flight was made on 26 February 1957 and it was piloted by "Monkey" Morgan and Max Conrad. Conrad was known as the flying grandfather who by his sixties had completed one hundred crossings of the Atlantic. The route was from Gander to Dublin. Capt. Morgan was killed in January the following year when he crashed in the Shannon estuary just after taking off from Shannon airport.

The show finished with a mass formation of all the aircraft taking part and the organisers estimated that a crowd of over 55,000 had attended the two day event.

Weston's 1958 show was moved to the Bank Holiday weekend 3 and 4 August. There were overcast skies, occasional showers and blustery winds representing the normal Summer weather profile in Ireland. The 808 which was the newest Viscount to enter the Aer Lingus fleet and capable of carrying sixty three passengers was piloted by Gordon Wade. He demonstrated high speed runs and steep turns before joining in formation with Darby Kennedy's DH84 Dragon EI-AFK to represent Aer Lingus old and new. The first Aer Lingus aircraft, the Dragon "Iolar" EI-ABI which operated the airline's inaugural flight in 1936 to Bristol, had been sold to Great Western and Southern Airlines on 30 June 1941. While flying from the Scilly Isles to Lands End EI-ABI disappeared without trace. It was presumed to have been shot down by a German JU88 which was active in the area at the time.

In 1967, after faithful service to Weston in the capable hands of Capt. Kennedy, who provided pleasure flights for the public both at the Weston displays and at other events around Ireland, Dragon EI-AFK was sold to Aer Lingus where it was painted up to represent the original "Iolar" EI-ABI and restored to flying condition.

Rene Vincent once again entertained the crowds with his rope ladder exploits while suspended from the Club's Auster which was travelling at a speed of 80 mph. at a height of 700 ft. Crop Culture Ltd. from the Isle of Wight demonstrated how the progressive farmer with a large acreage should be spraying his crops with the aid of a Tiger Moth. Officials of Bord na Mona (Irish Turf Company) and the Irish Sugar Company who were invited to attend the display were impressed. Some of the crowd did not share their enthusiasm, receiving an aerial rainshower from the spray equipment. The indomitable Freddy Bond performed a spectacular delayed opening parachute drop, a suitable finale to the fourth airshow at Weston organised by the Leinster Aero Club.

Because of the excellent exposure the demonstrated sports had received at the air displays, private and sport aviation were doing well. The Shamrock (Ireland) had got a parachute thanks to the efforts of Freddy Bond and his club members. The Irish Parachute Club had now trained twenty three members in the art of parachuting since its foundation in 1956 without incident. The Dublin Gliding Club had moved to Baldonnel to take advantage of its long runways and had three club training aircraft. Aero Modelling was at last recognised as not just of interest to children and had demonstrated the skill and expertise required to meet the exacting standards of both competitive and display flying.

The very success of the four big Weston shows dictated their downfall as the committee strived each year with a limited budget to get new and exciting acts. Bad gate receipts due to inclement weather had depleted the small resources so the July 1959 show was a modest event. It was called "Air Display and Parachute Rally" and was organised by the Leinster Aero Club, the Irish Parachute Club and the Dublin Gliding Club. Capt. Kennedy offered five shilling (25p) pay as you enter pleasure flights in the Dragon and many availed of this "once around the airfield" trip. Five thousand turned up on Sunday 19 July to see the action. The Parachute Club gave a demonstration of supply drops by parachute and Sgt. Peter Sheeran of the Air Corps and Thomas Lyng, an occupational therapist at Peamount Hospital, made their first jumps. They were presented with their wings by Mrs. Montgomery, widow of David Montgomery, cofounder of the Irish Parachute Club. The Gliding Club displayed their skill and expertise and a Turbulent Ultralight single engined monoplane assembled by the Rev. P.J. O'Kelly from Belfast was demonstrated by George Donoghue. Of unusual interest was the Percival Mew Gull G-AEXF flown to Weston by Peter Clifford of Exeter. Six of these aircraft were built and this was the only surviving example. AEXF was built in 1936 specifically for air racing. It was powered by a 210 hp. Gypsy Queen engine giving it a top speed of 230 knots. In 1937 Alex Henshaw won the King's Cup air race in this aircraft and in February 1939 AEXF was again the aircraft that enabled Henshaw to set the solo round trip record from London to Capetown, South Africa, a record which still stands to this day. AEXF was sold in France just before the war and eluded discovery by the Germans by being taken apart and stored in a number of barns in the area around Lyons. It was brought back to England in 1950 and Peter

Clifford raced the aircraft to victory in the King's Cup in 1955 at an average speed of 213 mph.

The Fokker Friendship delivered to Aer Lingus in November 1958 made its Airshow debut at Weston and was a fitting highlight to the show.

Demonstrations were given of supply drops by parachute. This idea had been pioneered by the Irish Parachute Club and would prove very effective during the harsh Winter of 1961/62 with supply drops to storm bound islanders off the coast and to snow bound villages in the Wicklow hills. The supply aircraft often flew with wingtips only feet from the mountain cliffs in order to get to the drop zones. Freddy Bond involved the Civil Defence instructor Noel O'Beara and Michael O'Gabhlainn, chief engineer, who had both made parachute jumps and were prime movers in this area. Their proud boast never having broken anything they dropped by parachute including a consignment of eggs and a complete kitchen sink.

On Sunday 23 July 1961 an air display and game fair was organised by the National Sport Association, the Dublin Gliding Club and the Irish Parachute Club. This was the first public display to be held at Baldonnel since the thirties. There were numerous side shows and sporting displays including gun dog demonstrations and private aircraft fly pasts. One of the female parachutists caused a stir when she had a parachute malfunction. Detta Gormley of Longford with twenty jumps to her credit had jumped from 2,000 ft. She had problems deploying her main chute and released her reserve. As she was now descending under two parachutes twisted together she had difficulty in manoeuvring to the target area and made a hard landing on the concrete runway. Thankfully she was unhurt. Ten thousand people attended. The admission was two shillings and sixpence (12.5p) and much to the relief of the organising committee, who had encountered unexpectedly heavy expenditure in creating the necessary facilities at Baldonnel, the event made a surplus of five pounds.

Two months later the Irish Parachute Club hosted its first truly international parachute display on Sunday 17 September at Weston. They were lucky with the weather as hurricane "Debbie" had passed over Ireland just twenty four hours earlier. Gusts of 160 mph. had been recorded in Belfast. The highlight of the display was the spectacular "Skydive", a delayed opening drop by three US Army parachutists who had travelled from their base in Wisbaden, Germany in their single engined Otter O 53312. This was the first time international parachutists appeared in Ireland at an airshow. The spot landing competition held in the afternoon was won by Dublin man Norman Hoffman. Second place was taken by Sgt. Chase, US Army, and third place went to Mike Reilly who was chairman of the parachuting section of the Royal Aero Club, London.

By now parachuting in Ireland had reached a stage where it was felt that it would benefit the sport if a team of Irish jumpers could be sent to represent Ireland at the Sixth World Sport Parachuting Championships. These events were to be held at Orange, Massachusetts in September 1962. To raise funds for this and to demonstrate competitive parachuting to the people of Cork, a display was planned for Sunday 22 July 1962 at Farmer's Cross. The airfield and facilities were provided free of charge by the Munster Aero Club and aircraft from Shannon and the Leinster Aero Club also took part. The Munster Motor Cycle and Car Club provided the traffic and perimeter patrol and Beamish and Crawford provided the hospitality, much of it the local brew. The army provided the tented village to house facilities required for the day.

The *Cork Examiner* Monday headline was "Skymen Cause Big Cork Traffic Jam". It was a beautiful day and the Cork people came out in their thousands. A continuous stream of cars made the trip up the hill to Farmer's Cross, situated just across the road from the present Cork Airport opened in October 1961. Farmer's Cross had served the city of Cork well as an aerodrome since 1934 and the Cork Aero Club operated from there until 1937 when the aircraft were sold and the club ceased operations. This Club had been an offshoot of the Irish Aero Club which went into liquidation that year bringing the Cork club with it. During the war years the field was closed and was lined with stakes to prevent an invasion force from landing. The much improved grass strip, 865 yds. in length, was officially opened in May 1948 and the reformed Cork Flying Club took up residence. Capt. Darby Kennedy of Weston provided many memorable pleasure flights for the citizens of Cork when he visited the field during the Summer months with his seven seater Dragon EI-AFK and eight seater DH89 Rapide EI-ADP.

Those who survived Cork's largest traffic jam were treated to an excellent display. Many bars along the route reported record takes as car owners cooled off in the heat. Over 9,000 people made it to the field. Johnny Gray, a founder member of the Cork Flying Club and an Air Traffic Control officer, suitably bedecked in straw hat and shorts, busily co-ordinated events on the ground and in the air. The Lord Mayor of Cork, Alderman Casey, opened the show and Freddy Bond, president of the Irish Aviation Club provided five and a half hours of continuous commentary. Six parachutists, men and women from the Irish team, competed with teams from the RAF skydivers club, the Green Jackets Parachute Club and the Scottish Parachute Club, as well as a couple of civilian parachutists from Austria and Holland. The RAF had offered to send an aircraft with their official display parachute team but permission from the Irish authorities was not forthcoming. The situation on the field got out of hand when crowds, who had parked their cars on the roadways around the field, came over the walls and rushed towards each parachutist as he was on his landing run. They did not seem to appreciate the danger they were in. One group, descending on a landing parachutist, was led in full flight by an old lady! One visiting parachutist declared to the local Press that "it was taking a far greater risk driving through the traffic on the way here than dropping by parachute onto the field". That was until the local crowds arrived. One parachutist was buried under a load of youngsters who had wanted to see this wonderous skyman in the flesh. Competitive jumping had to be abandoned for some time until the fields could be cleared. Meanwhile Hell Riders stunt motocycle teams under the leadership of Tom "Crash" Keegan performed various stunts including the thirty foot long tunnel of fire and the board wall crash.

At the end of the day the event had raised £1,700 towards the championship fund. This was to be the last event held at Farmer's Cross. The field was closed at the end of 1962 and was returned to crop. The Flying Club moved its operations to the airport across the road.

The Irish team at the World Championships consisted of five men and three women jumpers and was led by team manager Freddy Bond. Their enthusiastic jump aircraft pilot was Maurice Cronin of Leinster Aero Club. The team gained a lot of experience at the event and was placed seventh in the precision landing competition against very experienced opposition. They were competing against jumpers who individually would have had over 1500 jumps to their credit. To put this in perspective the sum total of the six Irish jumpers in the event was 1,000 jumps at that time.

35 Irish team at Orange, USA (left to right) Israeli competitor, Tommy Maloney, Tommy Lyng, Norman Hoffman, Jack McLoughlin, Mike Turner (masked behind McLoughlin), Mary Lawlor, Maurice Cronin, Freddie Bond

In County Meath Lord Headfort and some of his friends, all of whom were enthusiastic flying people got together in July 1962 and formed the Meath Flying Club. Six weeks later on 22 August they ran their first air display at a field in Headfort, just outside Kells. The display was officially opened by Erskine Childers who was then Minister for Transport and Power.

Three thousand people came to the show to see the many attractions including the Druine Turbulent formation team from the Tiger Club which was based in Redhill, Surrey. Lord Headfort was a member of this club. The team performed many stunts including flour bombing and cutting streamers. The Tiger Club had been formed in Redhill in 1956 by a handful of Tiger Moth enthusiasts to provide sport flying at the lowest possible cost. They performed their first team display in August 1959 and had appeared at several of the Farnborough air displays.

The tiny open cockpit single seater Turbulent was designed by Frenchman Roger Druine and built under licence by Rollason in England. Constructed of spruce and covered with fabric it was powered by a 1500 cc. VW engine and offered splendid manoeuvrability and economy. It was very much an ultralight aircraft with an empty weight of 400 lb., little more than the weight of a large motorbike. Fuel consumption was two and a half gallons per hour and it had a take off run of 350 ft. This was the Tiger Club's favourite aircraft for display and formation work.

Lord Headfort displayed the Czechoslovakian constructed Let Mraz Sokol M1C, three seater single engine monoplane, training and touring aircraft. Chipmunk No. 166 displayed for the Irish Air Corps. During the following week the Tiger Club and their aircraft accompanied by Lord Headfort in his Sokol, toured around the south of Ireland and visited the Shannon Aero Club at Coonagh airfield just outside Limerick city on Saturday 25 August. During the afternoon it was planned to fly a formation of aircraft over the city. In the late afternoon the formation of six Turbulents, a Jodel and the Sokol took to the air. Three aircraft from the Shannon Aero Club were to follow behind the main formation. Hundreds of people who were watching in the streets below as the formation flew overhead gasped in horror when the grey Taylorcraft EI-ALJ of the Shannon Aero Club flown by club member Joseph Selkirk collided with the red Turbulent G-ARIZ flown by twenty six year old Shaun de Salis. The tiny Turbulent was hit by the Taylorcraft's propeller from underneath damaging the Turbulent's wing and causing it to spin out of control. It crashed onto the Prospect Villas housing estate in the south end of the city and came to rest in the street beside the gable end of a house. De Salis was killed instantly. Miraculously there was no one else involved. The Taylorcraft glided down to Sarsfield barracks playing field with half the propeller gone and one wing damaged. The pilot steered the aircraft to a safe spot on the pitch clear of a soccer match in progress at the time. Selkirk, a native of Manchester, was taken to hospital with cuts to the face. EI-ALJ had joined the formation from the right without the knowledge of the Turbulent.

Messages of sympathy were sent on behalf of the people of Limerick by the Mayor, Mrs. Francis Condell, to the Salis family in England. Shaun de Salis was laid to rest in a private cemetery on the Stradbally estate, Co. Laois, where one of his aunts was buried. The rest of the team departed for England. It was a tragic end to their first visit to Ireland.

The Central flying group in Thurles held its first air display and rally at its newly opened field at Laffin just outside Thurles on Whitsun 2 June 1963. Rapide EI-AMN flown by Charlie O'Hara did the pleasure flying. Various light aircraft did flypasts and displays. Darby Kennedy's son Roger who later followed in his father's footsteps and became a pilot with Aer Lingus, flew Tiger Moth EI-AGP. An unusual aircraft EI-AKR, a chocolate and red coloured Bellanca 260, flown by Denis Greene and the only example of its type on the Irish register, had been delivered to Ireland in the middle of 1959 after a trans Atlantic ferry flight via the Azores. It was the demonstrator for the Irish and UK Bellanca agents. Cessna 185 Skywagon EI-AMT which was a six seater aircraft operated for Tara Exploration, was flown by Sam Pratt. He gave a demonstration of its short take off capabilities. EI-AMT was to crash on Lugnaquillia mountain, Co. Wicklow in June 1967.

Lord Headfort and the Meath Flying Group organised their second display at Headfort on Sunday 23 June 1963 and his friends from the Tiger Club joined him with their Turbulents and a Stampe. There were many flypasts featuring different aircraft. Members of the Irish Parachute Club and Dublin Gliding Club also gave displays. During the afternoon Lord Headfort presented the Shaun de Salis Memorial trophy to Short Brothers of Belfast. This trophy was created in memory of de Salis and awarded to organisations or individuals who have advanced the cause of aviation in Ireland.

The third display to be held at this venue was on Sunday 2 May 1965 and in spite of low cloud and rain, twenty three aircraft attended the event. The display opened with formation flying by three members of the Tiger Club who were once again loyally supporting the endeavours of the Meath Flying Group. They flew two Jodels and a Victa Airtourer. At 15.00 hrs. an Aer Lingus Boeing 707 performed several passes over the grass strip. The pilot had no difficulty finding the airfield in the low cloud since it operated the only radio beacon to exist at a private airfield in Ireland at that time. Pleasure flights were provided by two Cessnas operated

36 Turbulent flown by Shaun de Salis at Kells 1962,
prior to crash

by Pegasus Aviation. A gliding demonstration was given by the Dublin Gliding Club.

For just under thirty minutes a most interesting air sea rescue exercise by the Irish Air Corps gave the first public demonstration in Ireland of the new Alouette helicopter which had been delivered in November 1963. Lord Headfort also demonstrated the four seater Lake LA4 Amphibian for which he held the agency. This handy craft was capable of landing on both conventional runways and on water. It was powered by a single pusher engine located above the main fuselage.

On Sunday 6 June 1965 in a field one mile from Kilkenny, owned by local garage man John Hehir, an air day was organised by the National Campaign for Cancer Relief. The organising committee was headed by flying doctor Colm Killeen. Gay Byrne flew to Kilkenny with Colm in EI-AOD to open the display. Killeen was very impressed by Gay's flying skill and noted that the aircraft did not gain or lose even one hundred feet from the selected flight level during the whole trip. Gay had a great interest in aviation and had been taking flying lessons at Weston aerodrome. He went solo in 1964 and at that time had over sixty hours to his credit.

Events of the day included Arthur Wignall displaying aerobatics in a Tiger and an Air Corps helicopter display. Skydiving, gliding and model aircraft displays also took place. Fifty aircraft attended the event.

The next two displays which were held in a sleepy valley called Ballyfree in Glenealy, Co. Wicklow, were the first air displays I attended. I remember them with much affection as they made a favourable and lasting impression. This was the beginning of my love of aviation. I was completely hooked. The Phillips family on whose land the show was organised had to move a small hill and some trees on the eastern approach to the field before it could be licensed for use. After much improvement work the first show at Ballyfree was held in beautiful sunny weather at Whit, 3 and 4 June 1967. It was sponsored by Rothmans and was the first air display to be televised live by Telefis Eireann, the national television servie. TE broadcast a one hour segment each day. Pleasure flights were available to the public in helicopters and in a Piper Cherokee Six operated by Loganair of Glasgow. The morning programme featured over sixty aircraft arrivals from all parts of England and Europe to take part in the air rally and race.

Distinguished visitors to the display included Sir Alan Cobham who had done so much to make Ireland air minded in the thirties with his flying circus. He was acting as a member of the jury of appeals. The legendary air ace Group Capt. Douglas Bader and his wife arrived flying their own twin engined Beechcraft.

Recalling the air circuses of earlier days stunt lady Carol Koczon flew up and down the runway waving to the crowd while strapped to the wings of a Tiger Moth which was flown by Tiger Club pilot Robin Voice. This act demanded great skill as the drag created by the woman on the wing reduced the speed of the Moth close to stalling. The Rothmans Skydivers together with the Irish Sky Diving Club and the German Sky Diving team, made a lovely sight with their colourful parachutes and trailing smoke as they came in to land on the drop zone. The Rothmans team of seven jumped from their own Rapide 10,000 ft. over the field and while in free fall passed a baton between them before opening their 'chutes at 2,000 ft.

Tom Evans, a captain with Aer Lingus and first chairman of the newly reformed Irish Gliding Association, was given an aerotow by a powered air-craft flown by Mike Slazenger. Once launched, he gave a demonstration of the beauty of silent flight, flying the K6 glider. The most impressive part was his high speed flypast during which the K6 made a whistling sound as it sliced through the air. The Hughes 300 helicopter was demonstrated by Mike Smith of Transworld Helicopters. This company had been established in Shannon Airport in 1964 to act as agents for Hughes helicopters. They imported them from America for assembly and distribution to Europe. Transworld set up a training establishment for helicopter pilots. The company ceased operations in 1970.

Arthur Wignall who was very much involved in organising the Ballyfree display and was acting race controller, still found time to give a demonstration of aerobatic flight in a Stampe SV4C biplane, powered by a 140 hp. Renault engine. The vintage World War One replica biplanes used in the

37 Kilkenny Air Day 1965. Left to right, Marie Rowan, Ita and
Colm Killeen, Kathleen Watkins, Gay Byrne, Terry Rowan

38 Douglas Bader arrives at Ballyfree 1967

39 K6 Glider flown by Tom Evans, Ballyfree 1967

40 Carol Koczon "on the wing", Rothman's Display 1967

filming of *The Blue Max* made an interesting contrast. These three aeroplanes, led by Pat Cranfield, performed many of the dog fight sequences as seen on the film, with the red Fokker Triplane flown by John Hutchinson emerging the winner. The aircraft returned immediately after the display to Baldonnel where they were currently involved in the filming of *Darlin' Lily*, starring Julie Andrews and Rock Hudson.

On Sunday the international air race was run. It followed a triangular course around Co. Wicklow with turning points at Greystones and at Wicklow Head. Seventeen aircraft competed. The winner flying an Auster was Major E. Boylan of equestrian fame and a leading three day event rider. Major Boylan had over one thousand hours flying experience and was competing in his first rally and air race.

The 1968 Ballyfree display was also held on the Whit weekend 2 and 3 June. It offered a full day of aviation activity with something to please everyone, from the silence and beauty of glider flight, the true sailboats of the sky, to the gracious beauty of man's earliest form of aviation the balloon, to the roar of the 1500 hp. Rolls Royce Merlin engined P51 Mustang and the Air Corps two seat Vampire jet trainer. Parachute displays were much in prominence. Members of the Rothmans Skydiving team who were joined by a team of Irish Skydivers made a couple of drops during the afternoon after opening the show with a mass parachute drop. Parachutists from the Irish Skydiving Club, Tom Kellett and Bill Power, set a new Irish Parachuting record when they dropped from a height of 20,000 ft. during the afternoon. Neil Williams who had won the 1967 European aerobatic championships gave a most accomplished aerobatic display in his Zlin aircraft. Williams who was to become an aerobatic legend in his own lifetime died while flying a Heinkel from Spain to England in December 1977. The book he wrote on aerobatic flight is recognised as the standard work on the subject.

The last remaining Mustang in Europe which was used during World War Two as a high altitude interceptor and ground attack fighter bomber, did a most spectacular low level high speed run at around 400 knots down the runway and shattered the peace of the Co. Wicklow countryside. The all red mustang flown by twenty eight year old Charles Masefield had won the King's Cup Air Race in England in 1967. Thanks to the sponsorship from Rothmans over seventy two aircraft had been attracted to attend this international event and the winner of the Rally was English pilot Charles Strasser who had come in sixth place in 1967. The leading Irish entrant was Dr. Colm Killeen who had flown from San Sebastian to take twelfth place. Very much the flying doctor he used his aircraft for family holidays in Europe and to travel to international medical conferences. He got his licence in 1962 and had over four hundred hours flying experience. The air race which followed the same course as the previous year was postponed due to low cloud. On Monday the weather was better and the winner was London chartered accountant Tom Storey in a time of twenty eight minutes. Among the other interesting visitors to the rally was Piper Commanche 260 G-ATOY flown by famous air-woman Sheila Scott. Using this aircraft Sheila became the first British woman to fly solo around the world. She also held some forty other world records. Her aircraft, wearing racing number 99, carried testament to its travels with signatures inscribed on the fuselage from people all over the world.

The first hot air balloon of modern construction to appear in Ireland flew at the display on the Saturday. The orange coloured MBl 65,000 cu. ft. balloon was only the second of the type to be manufactured in England and the sport was very much in its infancy. It was flown on the day by English pilot Bill Malpas. It took off and disappeared over the hills to land safely in the next valley. Anthony Smith brought along his silver coloured 18,000 cu. ft. hydrogen balloon and Irish Industrial Gases were persuaded by display organiser Tim Phillips to part with £250 worth of hydrogen free of charge to inflate it. On Sunday afternoon Anthony Smith finished the inflation which took eight hours to complete. He invited Christopher Martin, secretary of the Irish Aviation Club, to accompany him as a passenger. Christopher remembers pilot Smith mischievously calling out to the populous underneath as they drifted silently over the Wicklow countryside, "Is this the right way to France?". A successful landing was made soon afterwards.

Shortly after this historic event the Dublin Ballooning Club held its inaugural meeting under the chairmanship of Maurice Cronin. The club received delivery of its first hot air balloon in 1969 and Maurice became the first Irishman to qualify as a hot air balloon pilot.

By five o'clock on Sunday evening all the aircraft were going home, taking off into a clear blue sky. There had been over ninety different types parked on the field including Chipmunks, Beagles, Cessnas and Cherokees. A few hours later only a grass field remained, silent and empty.

A small "around Ireland rally" and race was held on 24 and 25 May 1969. Aircraft travelled from Ballyfree to Castlebar and back. Tim Phillips now turned his hand to competitive air racing on the international circuit and was to take part along with his good friend Vyrell Mitchell in the non-stop London to Sydney air race in December 1969. He came fourth in a time of sixty seven hours. In Summer 1971 flying a twin engined Piper Commanche EI-AVD in the London to Victoria BC Canada race he won his class and came second overall out of a field of seventy nine. To-day he manages Ballyfree Farms in Co. Wicklow.

41 Neil Williams in the Zlin, Ballyfree 1968

42 P51 Mustang displayed by Charles Masefield, Ballyfree 1968

By the early seventies air displays were commonplace. They were being held all around the country during the Summer months and were drawing on the many sporting bodies now in existence for their display items. On Sunday 15 August 1971 a fly in and display was organised by the Abbeyshrule Development Company, Co. Longford. It was to become Ireland's longest running air display. Abbeyshrule has hosted a show every year since then and gets loyal support from both the local and the national aviation community. It is traditionally held in early August and aviators are assured of a friendly welcome and great hospitality. In its shows over the years it has featured all facets of aviation: military participation by the Air Corps; commercial demonstrations from Avair 330, Aer Turas Britannia, Aer Lingus 747 and Ryan Air's BAC 111; various aerobatic performances from among others, Roy Legge, Brian Lecomber and our own Arthur Wignall. Unusual acts like G-HUNT, the Hunter jet and an all red Spitfire have also appeared as well as the Hawker Sea Fury, Ken Wallis and "Little Nellie" and a Pilatus P2. In 1980 the Royal Jordanian Falcons flying their three Pitts Specials gave their only display in Ireland at Abbeyshrule.

Jim Byrne on whose land the original airfield stood had been welcoming aviators to Abbeyshrule since it first opened in 1957. On 20 September 1977 tragedy struck the aviation community when he and two other founder members of the Abbeyshrule Aero Club, Tom Gannon and Dick Reilly were killed when their aircraft struck a mountain as they were returning from a flying rally at Kilbrittain, Co. Cork in bad weather conditions.

It was decided by the remaining members that, despite the tragedy, aviation should continue in Abbeyshrule and landowners Mr. Edward McGoey and Mr. Bertie Mills provided a new site for the airfield half a mile from the village. After a lot of hard work the new field was opened in time for their seventh annual display in August 1977.

In 1979 an asphalt runway replaced the grass strip. The Smurfit executive Lear jet did the first jet touch and go at this display. Despite the tragedy, the setbacks and the bad weather, Ted McGoey, Sammy Bruton and the committee seem determined to keep the show running for many more years and to keep alive "the friendliest show in the midlands".

The Kerry county airport was opened at Farranfore in 1969. It had a tarmac runway of 1,100 metres. Before long they were organising their first event which was an air race on 3 and 4 June 1972. This developed into an International rally and air display over the years until their last display in 1984. Many exciting items appeared during that time including microlights, parachutists, formation flying with the Vixen Two, a YAK 11, a DC3, a Gyrocopter and Air Corps displays.

In August 1984 they featured a real coup for Irish air displays when the Air France Concorde which was on route to Shannon airport for a five week training detail appeared and much to the amazement of the crowd did a high speed and a low speed flypast. At one point the Concorde undercarriage was within feet of touching the runway before the captain applied full throttle and soon left Farranfore far below. Breathtaking.

Weston had a display in September 1981 to celebrate the opening of the new 3,000 ft. tarmac runway which started a new era for Capt. Kennedy and his most successful long running flying school. There had been an airfield at Weston since 1938. Kennedy took to the air in a thirty-eight year old Tiger Moth to show that he had not lost the magic touch. Pearse Cahill who owns Dublin's other flying school "Iona" which is based at Dublin airport demonstrated the true spirit of aviation when he arrived over the airfield towing a banner which said "Good Luck Weston".

On 22 July 1984 Coonagh airfield just outside Limerick city held the first air display to be seen in the mid western region since 1957. Airfields at Carrickfin, Co. Donegal, Sligo, Castlebar and Galway have all held displays over the last few years. Aerodromes and air displays are now commonplace in Ireland, a far cry from the humble beginnings at the racecourse in Leopardstown in 1910.

43 Air Corps Marchetti team, Abbeyshrule

3
Going to the Races

44 Handbill for first Fairyhouse display

The dismal results of a raffle run by the Irish Aviation Club was one of the main reasons for the creation of Air Spectacular, the air display which became Ireland's international air show, thanks to the dedicated work of the voluntary committees of the IAC. Little did one dream in 1977 that Air Spectacular would become such a huge success.

During the Summer of 1977 it became obvious to the board of the IAC that if further progress was to be made in fostering sporting aviation, a steady regular annual source of funds would have to be found. The IAC had depended on subscriptions from the affiliated associations and on administration subvention from Aer Rianta. Aer Rianta was established by government in 1937 to administer airports in Ireland. Its first chairman, Sean O hUadhaigh, had close links with the Irish Aviation Club. Aer Rianta's constitution gave it responsibility to encourage the development of all forms of aviation including sport aviation and in the fifties Aer Rianta had accomplished this through its air education section. It very much saw the Irish Aviation Club as being in a position to foster sporting aviation in the seventies.

Ballooning had just re-affiliated to the IAC having resolved a minor financial crisis of its own. I was not long secretary of the Dublin Ballooning Club when I began to attend the IAC's board meetings on the Ballooning Club's behalf. I still had a close informal contact with the IAC having been a member of the organising committee for the FAI conference, hosted by the IAC, in Dublin in 1973. Fund raising was central at those IAC board meetings and various suggestions and strategies for raising money were proposed. A raffle had been run over the Summer months which in fact had lost money. Drastic measures were called for. Fund raising was on the agenda afresh for the September 1977 meeting. Various ideas were examined that night, coffee mornings, bring and buy sales and so on. I suggested that we organise an event incorporating our skills as aviators, something we were bound to be at home with, an air display. The board felt the idea had some merit and it was decided to form a sub-committee. Since I had made the suggestion I was given the job of organising secretary. That job was to continue for ten long years. The perks of organising secretary are two in number. Firstly, you organise an air display, an interesting challenge. Secondly, you can book acts and aircraft types which are not normally seen in Ireland. The drawbacks are many. For a year's hard work you get not one penny. Summer holidays before September are out of the question. Long anti-social hours and no complaints tolerated. What kept me going? Well, I had never done anything like this before. I would have a go and show a bit of confidence in the idea.

The show date was to be Sunday 27 August 1978 and Christopher Martin, then IAC secretary, suggested the title "Air Spectacular 78". The Model Aeronautics Council had run some very successful model competitions and flying displays at a racetrack called Fairyhouse in Co. Meath. Fairyhouse was a good site with ready made facilities, toilets, catering block and grand stands. The grass finishing straight was an ideal runway. In fact Fairyhouse had served for years as a landing strip, the centre area had been used for training by local aero clubs.

Jockey Dan Moore who lived nearby first operated a Miles Messenger single engined aircraft from there in 1948. Moore, who was Maurice Cronin's favourite uncle, had given him his first aeroplane flight. When the Leinster Aero Club needed a new training area, Maurice suggested Fairyhouse. The field was first licensed in 1965.

History was repeating itself. The controlling body for sport aviation was about to set up an air display at a famous Irish racecourse. The first meeting of the organising committee was held at chairman Tom Farrington's offices at 106 Pembroke Road, Ballsbridge, Dublin. An agreement was drawn up with Fairyhouse. The show was on the road but what a list there was. Aeroplanes and their control we could handle but the many other nitty gritty items like hygiene requirements, crowd control, traffic flow, car parking, litter, catering concessions, show programme production, cash collection and publicity were outside our normal range of activities. The committee was on a learning curve and the list seemed endless. The assorted talents within the club were urgently called upon. Chris Bruton who had been involved with aviation since the early thirties

and who had been the first secretary of the Junior National Aviation Club
could advise us on his past experiences with other displays. He had been
a commentator at many of them. Norman Colfer, the manager at Fairyhouse, joined the committee and gave valuable advice on the local scene.

Christopher Martin, vice-chairman, took on the show insurance and
the financial aspects with Charles Orme, IAC treasurer. Tom Kellett of
the Parachute Association got public relations. Bill Howarth, a captain
with Aer Lingus and CFI of the Leinster Aero Club, would arrange the
licensing of the field with the Department of Transport and give the
safety briefings to pilots on the day. Peter Hynes, an air traffic controller by profession and a glider pilot on his days off, advised on air
traffic control with his colleague Liam McCobb. Phil Haycock, a private
pilot who had done trojan work for the IAC's air education programme,
was appointed manager of flying on the day.

My task was to get suitable acts with which to fill the programme. I
had a shoe string budget of £500. I wrote to Maurice Cronin, a kingpin
of Irish sport aviation and close to the aviation grapevine. Could he recom-
mend an aerobatic display pilot who was professional, safe in flight and
a good entertainer? His immediate reply was Brian Lecomber. Brian was
an up and coming British pilot who was asking £250 for a display. We
booked him straight away. He had the honour of being the first aerobatic
pilot to display at Fairyhouse. I phoned Brian to confirm the booking and
to give him details of the venue. When I told him the display would take
place on a horse racing track he knew not what to expect. Not having
been to Ireland he was unsure how to deal with the "crazy Irish". He
was to be pleasantly surprised.

Drawing on my contacts in the ballooning world I discovered that the
Robertson's Jams hot air balloon, in the shape of a huge Golly, was
available. The sponsor was willing to bring this special shape to Dublin,
the first time it would be seen in Irish skies. As a balloonist I looked forward to seeing Golly even though the odds were against it being able to
make a successful flight. The weather in Ireland is not often kind to ballooning which requires light winds and dry conditions. Also the shelter
at Fairyhouse was poor. I had my fingers crossed.

There were two problems with the landing area which had to be resolved
before the Department would issue the necessary licence. The first was a
thirty foot camera tower set to one side of the main straight which was to
be our runway. Dunlop lent us one mile of their yellow bunting with which
we decorated the tower making it so obvious that even a bat could see it
and this resolved the problem. There were two fixed jumps on the straight.
These constituted our second problem. Norman Colfer resolved this by
sawing the jumps in half, removing them for the display, then rebuilding

them afterwards. My Summer was very busy seeking out affordable acts, co-ordinating arrangements in hand and haggling for the best possible deals. Perforce I became a "hard woman to deal with". As Air Spectacular was an unknown quantity, selling advertising in the show programme and organising sponsorship of the display acts was hard graft. Customers were not exactly rushing forward with wads of money in their hands. Still we were learning. Final preparations to the runway strip were completed the day before the show. Fairyhouse "International" was a hive of activity as equipment was installed and tested, static exhibits moved into place and hundreds of other jobs brought to completion. During the afternoon I collected our aerobatic star Brian Lecomber at Dublin Airport and took him across to Fairyhouse by car for a close look at the display site. He was impressed by what he had seen of the Irish countryside so far during his sunny afternoon flight from Castlebridge airfield in Wexford where he had landed to clear customs. From his open cockpit biplane he became enthralled by the beautiful scenery, the fresh colours and tiny villages, unlike anything he was used to in England. He found himself sinking lower and lower as he absorbed the unfolding beauty below.

45 Golly

When he saw the track his reservations disappeared and he was loud in his praise. He felt it was a superb place for a small display in a rural setting with good facilities for the crowds. It was wonderfully odd to have aeroplanes sitting on the ground in front of the grand stands. Fairyhouse was to become one of his favourite airshows. When he returned to England news of the Irish racetrack Air Spectacular soon spread and interest was high. He stayed overnight at our house and we found him to be a most down to earth person, for an aerobatic pilot. We soon resolved the problem of what to give him for breakfast. "Just a glass of orange juice please", sez Brian, "a few rashers, a sausage or two, an egg, tomato, toast and a few cups of coffee to wash it all down." A true aerobatic breakfast, bearing in mind the punishment it would be subjected to in a couple of hours. Brian Lecomber — nice person. We all benefited from his company.

The historic day for the IAC dawned slightly overcast and with light winds. By the start time of 14.30 hrs. the Irish Aviation Club had embarked on the air display business for the first time. The crowd looked a respectable size thanks to good weather and advertising and the gate had passed the break even point. The committee was feeling good. All that remained was to give the audience a good show. Brian Lecomber rolled off in the first slot, in his orange and blue Stampe, to open Air Spectacular '78.

Low cloud prevented the Irish Parachute Association display team from creating a new Irish record with a nine man link up free fall from 12,000 ft. They had to make do with a low level drop from the Aer Arran Islander and were tracking across the skies at 150 knots. The parachutists were flying the very advanced square shaped canopies which closely resemble flying wings.

As conditions remained calm man's earliest aerial chariots took to the air. The Dublin Ballooning Club's training balloon EI-BBM was flown by David Hooper CFI, also an instructor with the Gliding Club. David became a hot air balloon pilot in 1969. The Robertson's Jams special shape golly balloon G-OLLI stood over ninety feet tall when inflated by its pilot Tom Sage from England. Tom was no stranger to Ireland having flown at the national ballooning championships, held every year in Co. Longford.

One of the trickiest acts of the afternoon was the hang glider drop from balloon. This was the first demonstration of the act at a public event and only the second time it was attempted in Ireland. The pilot John Harris from Dublin together with his hang glider was carried to a height of 2,000 ft. slung underneath hot air balloon EI-BAN flown by Mike Alexander, a captain with Aer Lingus. Harris was released by cutting the rope with a knife. The glider dropped sharply before stabilising and much to our relief made a safe landing in front of the crowd.

Brian Lecomber's second act was a crazy flying routine during which he demonstrated all sorts of aerial wobbles and ended up by skillfully hopping the fences on the racetrack. The crowd loved it and applauded loudly. He waggled his wings in farewell and headed for Birr, Co. Offaly, for a display as part of Birr vintage week festivities. Finding Birr presented an unexpected problem until he spotted a brightly coloured hot air balloon. He rightly concluded that he would find an air display underneath. When he landed and parked his aircraft the crowd swarmed around it only to be held at bay by a marshal brandishing a fire extinguisher. Brian was amused by this novel technique of crowd control.

Meanwhile back at Fairyhouse the passengers on board Aer Lingus flight 166 from Dublin to Heathrow got a pleasant surprise when their 737 did a flypast as part of the display. The pace of the show slowed markedly for a time as Aer Lingus insisted that all traffic at Fairyhouse be grounded before the 737 left Dublin airport. One enthusiast, bored by the delay, expressed his disappointment that the 737 did not perform a loop. The Press reported that 10,000 people attended the three hour display. We had checked, 4,500 adults and 3,200 children through the slow moving turnstiles. We later discovered that a further 2,000 had got in scot free to an unmanned and closed car park at the bottom end of the racecourse.

The Aer Arran Islander provided the pleasure flights and its pilot Paddy Robinson, who normally flies the ten seat commuter between the Aran Islands and Galway, was kept very busy before and after the show. Air Spectacular '78 made a profit of £1,472 which was shared equally with Fairyhouse. The IAC's share of £736 was distributed among the affiliated sporting groups and was a welcome bonus encouraging everyone to make even greater efforts for next year. In early September we held the wrap-up meeting and had a hard look at possible improvements. Our first air display had turned out well and we had learned a lot about display organising. At the next board meeting we agreed unanimously on another display in 1979. Club president Tom Hudson and myself were asked to form an organising committee and to set the date. We decided to keep the committee small on the basis that a tight dedicated team is more effective than a diversity of volunteers, borne out over the years as a sound principle. The committee members became in turn team leaders who formed sub-committees to cover their area of responsibility. Progress was reported to the main IAC monthly board meetings. The commitee for Air Spectacular '79 welcomed some new hands on board. Tom Hudson took up the responsibility for ground services. Terry Rowan was appointed air display director and field manager in charge of security. Tony

46 Air Arran Islander

Leonard, of the Aircraft Owners and Pilots Association, agreed to develop a competitive input to the show to encourage private pilots to attend. Dr. Colm Killeen was appointed air display medical officer while Peter Hynes and Liam McCobb once again became our air traffic controllers.

Display director Terry Rowan had long been a campaigner for the cause of sporting aviation and for the IAC in particular since 1967 when he first served as president. He was now serving as vice-president to the international aviation sporting body, the FAI. Our medical director Dr. Killeen had also been with the IAC since 1967 and represented Ireland on the FAI international medical committee. He had given me my first trip in a light aircraft in the Winter of 1971 when I was treated to some circuits at night in his Cessna 182 at Dublin Airport. Sadly the IAC was to lose the services and expertise of secretary Christopher Martin who after thirteen years was leaving the club.

Finance for the display was still a major concern and once again I launched into phone calls and letters to companies I thought might be interested. My job was made a little easier with one successful show to refer to. In March 1979 I received a call from Ronan Power, sales development manager, British Airways. He expressed an interest in the show and asked for a meeting. This followed and we reported back to the board. Thus began a three year agreement with British Airways as overall sponsor of Air Spectacular. It was the beginning of a long, fruitful and happy association. The IAC was very pleased to welcome British Airways as the prime sponsor of Air Spectacular. BA had identified a business opportunity and were willing to provide the necessary financial input just at the right time.

To extend the show's interest among the general aviation community as well as the public, we discussed broadening the display to include Birr. We met the chairman of the Midland Flying Club, John Irwin, just before Christmas 1978 to discuss running one show on Saturday at Birr to tie in with vintage week and to follow on with Air Spectacular at Fairyhouse on Sunday. We would share the display acts and both groups would thus benefit from shared fuel and transit charges on aircraft from the UK. On 14 January 1979 John Irwin took off from Birr airfield with parachutists on board for a practice drop. The Piper aircraft crashed killing John and three parachutists including Michael Flaherty, who had for many years been CFI of the Irish Parachute Club. Michael had gone to Birr that weekend to help form a local parachute club. He had been one of the team who had jumped at Air Spectacular '78 and had been a guiding light in the sport of parachuting.

In early 1979 the Irish Aviation Club became the Irish Aviation Council. The board felt that this name would be more descriptive of its modern role. It no longer operated aircraft for club use and was more a representative body or council for sporting aviation in Ireland.

The international oil crisis brought a temporary shortage of petrol in Ireland during the Spring of 1979. Petrol rationing was introduced for a short time and it looked likely that Air Spectacular '79 would have to be cancelled. Thankfully the supply had returned to normal by August. A budget of £1,000 was allocated for acts. We booked Roy Legge from Kent to give the aerobatic display. Roy was well known in Ireland for some memorable displays at Abbeyshrule over the years.

Tom Hudson, who was very much involved in the sport of hang gliding and had been instrumental in starting it in Ireland in 1973, had unearthed a zany young Scotsman from Kilmarnock called Jim Potts. We immediately christened him McPotty. McPotty had made history for the sport by crossing from Scotland to Northern Ireland in June 1979 suspended beneath his hang glider, which was powered by a 110 cc. modified Chrysler outboard motor unit driving a pusher propeller. McPotty's sophisticated throttle lever was a huge spring clothes peg which he held in his mouth. Bite hard on the peg and the engine speeded up, release the pressure and the engine slowed down. In an emergency, to cut the engine you spat out the peg. The McPotty throttle was elegant in its simplicity but coughing or even a delicate yawn were out, a sneeze could have alarming results. McPotty's antics during the Air Spectacular '79 weekend provided a lot of light relief. It was great to get a few laughs in the organised chaos of the airshow. McPotty enjoyed his sport and showed great skill in demonstrating this new form of flight, which was in reality the forerunner of the present day Microlight. During his hang gliding days he had a nerve shattering experience in mid-air when his bottom control bar broke in half. He held the pieces together and made an emergency landing. McPotty lives to fly another day, a true entertainer.

One week before the show British Airways brought its mobile exhibition unit on tour to Dublin, Cork, Limerick, Kilkenny, Birr and finally Fairyhouse where it was open to the public during the show. The exhibition, mounted on a forty foot trailer, featured a mock-up flight deck of a Boeing 747 Jumbo Jet. The Lord Mayor of Dublin opened the tour on Saturday 18 August at the Mansion House. We decided to have a parade through the city starting from Parnell Street. A small convoy of trucks and cars demonstrated the various sport aviation activities available. A glider was rigged on one trailer. I was on another with a parachute on my back waving to the bemused Saturday shoppers. My husband Colm, a hot air balloon pilot, towed a trailer by car with a fully rigged balloon basket and burner on board. David Hooper was standing in the basket operating the burner, blasting away at regular intervals. The ITGWU band led the parade followed by the British Airways marching majorettes, leggy and with twirling batons. Along the parade route girls distributed leaflets about Air Spectacular. By the time the parade had reached St. Stephen's Green a litter warden was hard on our heels, looking for somebody in authority. He finally spotted the Lord Mayor's car carrying Danny Nickson, sales promotion manager of British Airways, Ronan Power and of course the Lord Mayor himself. The warden tapped on the window and demanded to know who was going to pick up all this rubbish being given out.

The weather on Sunday 26 August was perfect. There was just enough wispy cloud to soften the glare of the sun. Twenty thousand people turned up to see the action. The gates were opened at eleven o'clock and the queues quickly formed for pleasure flights in the Aer Arran Islander. Queues also formed to see the 747 mock-up flight deck. The winner of our "VIP for a Day" competition on RTE's Radio 2 programme "Poperama" was soon aboard the British Airways Rapide enjoying his prizewinning flight. This Rapide G-AKOE which had been built for the RAF in 1942 and had served with them until 1964 was painted in British Airways colours to commemorate the fact that this type had been in service with BEA (British European Airways) until the early sixties. Flown by Sqn. Ldr. Dick Milliard it had come in from Liverpool on Sunday morning. The Rapide has a cruising speed of 120 mph. Among the eight passengers was one of the show commentators, Bob Danvers Walker, a well known commentator on BBC Radio and Television and a true gentleman. Bob was quite an achiever and his accomplishments included walking a high wire and diving with Jacques Cousteau. He had only the briefest time for a quick read through the show information, which I had dumped on him, before joining Chris Bruton in the commentary box. By 13.00 hrs. the rush was on in earnest and our new cash collection system was working well. Paddy Byrne, a newcomer to the council, did the trouble shooting during the day. Paddy was a member of the Society of Amateur Aircraft Constructors and was building his own aircraft in his spare time.

In the static display park we had a homebuilt Evans VP1 EI-AYY powered by a 1500 cc. engine. It had a range of 150 miles and a cruising speed of 75 mph. This aircraft took computer executive Mick Donoghue four years to construct and it was Ireland's first single seat homebuilt to fly. EI-AYY was displayed at the show by John O'Loughlin CFI of the Wexford Aero Club who had test flown it in April 1976.

The display director Terry Rowan, myself as show co-ordinator and our support team were located on the far side of the runway from the grandstand and controlled the display from the race starter's mobile box. The box was connected by telephone to Dublin air traffic control using a

47 Powered Hang-glider flown by Jim Potts, Fairyhouse 1979

radio link as a back up. The telephone connection was a source of worry in the early years at Fairyhouse as the service was temperamental. It was however a great improvement on the system we had used the previous year at Fairyhouse when controller Liam McCobb had stood among the crowd high in the open stand operating the radio while Peter Hynes hung about in the general enclosure, with a pocketful of 10p coins, within striking distance of a public telephone box and Dublin ATC.

The show briefing for participating pilots was at 13.30 hrs. By that time one had run a marathon all over Fairyhouse chasing aircrew passes for pilots, lunch vouchers, arranging last minute changes of slot times and the host of other details.

After the timed arrival competition was completed the main show opened at 14.30 hrs. as IAC president Tom Hudson fired a flare. The first item was a single high speed fly past of Tom Farrington's twin engined Cessna 414 flown by USAF veteran John Coltan. The ideal weather meant that all thirty five parachutists from the Irish Parachute Association were able to jump from the Clyden DC3 EI-BDU. They took twenty seconds to exit from the aircraft. It was the biggest mass parachute drop in Ireland.

Roy Legge flying his Bucker Jungmeister carried off the Marlboro trophy for the best vintage aircraft in attendance. This single seat aerobatic tourer was first flown in 1935. Legge's trademark was his one and a half flick roll from knife edge to knife edge. The Jungmeister was a popular aircraft for aerobatics in the nineteen thirties and early forties. Its controls were light and precise particularly in the rolling plane. Legge died the following year while practising for the next display season in his new aircraft a Zlin. He suffered a heart attack while at the controls.

The Air Corps was out in force with a recruiting campaign and static exhibit of aircraft on the ground. They had an aerial display of helicopter, fixed wing Marchettis and the four Fouga jets which screamed by at over 300 mph. Our gritty Scotsman Jimmy Potts who had done two practice runs during the morning with no problems now took off in his powered hang glider. Suddenly the wasp-like sound of his engine went silent. He tried to restart in flight but it refused to co-operate and he had to land. Unfortunately the programme was running behind time and we were unable to give him a second slot. Potts moaned dejectedly, "I think I'll go and have a wee cry."

Another disappointment was the British Airways Boeing 747 Jumbo which was unable to take off. This Jumbo was the 12 ft. 6 in. scale model version which had arrived from England in a trailer. The two and a half inch wheels were supporting a weight of 56 lb. and as the going was soft they got bogged down in the grass so the 747 was unable to reach its lift off speed of 65 mph. The giant model, the then biggest in the world, normally flew from concrete runways. The team of six pilots and ground crew who travelled with it were most disappointed. It was the first time that a Boeing 747 was ever grounded due to the length of the grass.

Aer Lingus Captain John Hutchinson displayed one of the vintage aircraft that had starred in the film *The Blue Max* which was shot in Ireland. This was the Morane-Saulnier MS 230 Parasol EI-ARG. It was built in 1929 and had served with the French and Belgian air forces in the mid-thirties. John required all his skills to fly this aircraft because of a tendency to ground loop on landing. This nasty habit had killed a lot of pilots over the years.

Thanks to calm conditions all the hot air balloons were able to inflate and the public were treated to the rare sight of four Irish registered balloons in flight. Purple coloured EI-BAN, a Cameron 65, once again carried hang glider pilot Johnny Harris aloft this time to a height of 7,000 ft. before cutting the rope. Johnny soared above the balloon and availed of the lift from the venting hot air coming off the top of the balloon. He then spiralled down closely following the balloon's descent.

The Press reported next day that the air display had been a high flying air spectacular.

During the year the IAC had nominated me for the position of Hon. Secretary to the council, a position I declined since I had a similar post

48 Homebuilt VP1 flown by John O'Loughlin

50 The Morane-Saulnier MS230 Parasol flown
by John Hutchinson

49 Balloon and Hang-glider

with the Dublin Ballooning Club. This plus Air Spectacular, plus my normal family activities, was leaving just not enough hours to go around. At the winding-up meeting we welcomed Paddy Byrne on to the main display committee and generally came to the conclusion that our workforce was being stretched. For 1980 we would need to find more willing volunteers. On the positive side we made a modest profit of £1,200 for the IAC and British Airways had guaranteed its sponsorship for a further two years. Just before Christmas it was realised that due to possible major construction work at Fairyhouse the venue might not be available for the 1980 Air Spectacular. We immediately began investigating suitable alternatives including our old friend Leopardstown Racecourse. This was quickly deleted from the list due to obstacles in the flight path and the recent spate of development in the area.

January passed with no success. In February Norman Colfer called to say that the proposed development work at Fairyhouse would not be as extensive as first envisaged so the course would be available for the air display in August. Sighs of relief all round. The date for Air Spectacular '80 was set for Sunday 17 August and we got down to work.

The commentary team for 1980 was expanded and now consisted of Mike Kelly, who was acting Public Relations Officer for the IAC, Chris Bruton, Capt. Joe Dible and John Blake, famous for his commentaries at Farnborough.

One of the first tasks for the new IAC secretary Peter Costello was to organise a small VIP reception to be held in one of the catering areas during the day. This was to thank in a positive way the sponsors and the individuals who had helped the show and the IAC over the year. A ladies committee was formed to take care of the catering. Many a cupboard and fridge in committee members' homes was bare that weekend in the cause of furnishing a most successful buffet lunch after which the guests took their places in the grandstand to enjoy the show. The lunch became an annual event. We had to be watchful of gate crashers it became so popular. Needless to say the organising committee never got near the place as 12.30 hrs. was the frantic time. Liam McCobb's wife Anne produced the perfect solution, a huge juicy melon. Easy to eat when you are on the move and most refreshing. It was to become the traditional lunch on the Air Control side of the track. Anne faithfully supplied this delicacy every year and it even appeared out of the murk in Cork in 1985.

The show briefing was held in the jockey's weigh-in room, much to the amusement of the pilots who loved the intimacy and atmosphere that was Fairyhouse.

Thanks to the efforts of the British Airways publicity machine, advertising for the show was reaching a much wider audience. Twelve thousand handbills had been given out at the Horse Show in the RDS Dublin two weeks earlier. We also expanded the Press and Radio competitions with novelty items including a little Miss Air Spectacular. It worked. Over 30,000 people flocked to see the show. The *Evening Herald* correspondent in his report stated that "the Irish have gone mad on the air. . . . The road to Air Spectacular '80 was choked with cars. All the air mad Irish had combined to bring their enthusiasm to one place. All I can ask is what about the recession?" Perhaps people could not resist the colour and the excitement of an air display to brighten their day. With so many things to see even the ominous clouds and heavy showers of the day failed to dampen their spirits.

The show was led by the star attraction Sally B, a B17 World War Two bomber whose massive four engines purred gently as it made slow and fast flypasts of the course. Sally B is one of the last airworthy examples of this type in the world and is dedicated to the memory of the 79,000 US airmen who were killed in the flame torn skies over Europe between 1942 and 1945. As Fairyhouse was a small grass strip the B17 could not land but Vampire WZ 507 did touch the grass and went into history as the first jet aircraft movement ever to be recorded on an Irish racecourse. The pilot was Scotsman John Turnbull. Seeing the Vampire in action brought back many nostalgic memories to those members of the Irish Air

51 "Sally B"

52   Vampire WZ507 flown by John Turnbull

Corps who had flown them in the fifties. As a matter of interest the second recorded jet movement on an Irish racetrack was at Midleton, Co. Cork, on 18 April 1983 when a Mexican registered executive jet landed short of fuel. A special tarmac runway had to be built to allow it to take off again.

Air Corps engineer Capt. Graham Liddy swopped cockpits for the day and gave a star performance in his Astir glider. Graham was a senior gliding instructor with the Dublin Gliding Club and he was towed into the air by the DGC chief tug pilot David Hooper in the Piper Super Cub. On release at 3,000 ft. the glider executed a series of loops, chandells and stall turns before finishing with a high speed low level pass in front of the grandstands followed by a loop which seemed to bottom out only feet above the ground, then a perfect landing to rapturous applause.

The weather did affect some of the acts. The planned mass drop of thirty five parachutists from the DC3 was reduced to the ten most experienced jumpers who braved the conditions and landed safely. The special shape hot air balloon created to represent a spark plug remained in its bag as did its colleagues. It was much too windy for ballooning. Two Harvard World War Two training aircraft which were routing to Fairyhouse from Valley in North Wales had to turn back due to low cloud which came down to 700 ft. in the Irish Sea. Most vintage aircraft are equipped to fly in visual flight conditions only and do not carry the range of instruments necessary to enable safe flight through cloud.

Thankfully we had a packed programme so these losses did not affect the show content. The Irish Independent Commuter Airline Avair, which had sponsored the B17 appearance at the show set up a large and interesting static exhibit. Avair also demonstrated its King Air and Beechcraft Skipper aircraft. Pierce Cahill's son Peter continued the tradition of Iona National Airways' longstanding connections with Irish air displays by demonstrating the Cessna twin engined 414 EI-BGP. Flightline's Rockwell 690 gave high speed and low speed flypasts and finished with a landing. The Air Corps introduced the Gazelle helicopter to the Irish public. It had been delivered to the service earlier in the year.

Aer Lingus pilot Neil Johnson gave an aerobatic display in his Falco which was fitted with smoke. Neil, from Ballymena in Northern Ireland, flies Boeing 737s on the Aer Lingus European routes. He is a former national aerobatic champion. His wife Grainne is also an Aer Lingus pilot and has the distinction of being its first woman pilot. British Airways Tri-Star captain John Kitchin brought over the Campbell Gyroplane G-AXVK which is powered by a 2074 cc. engine. He gave a demonstration of hands off flying by sticking his hands out and waving to the crowd. A curious blackbird flying alongside would have noticed that his knees were white with the effort of holding the control stick in the straight and level position. The gyroplane was not an easy aircraft to fly and had a savage sting in the tail awaiting the unwary pilot. A similar machine crashed in front of thousands of spectators at Farnborough in 1970 killing the pilot, "Pee Wee" Hunt. Kitchin himself had a close call in September 1978 when a gust of wind overturned the gyroplane while landing during a display at RAF Abingdon. Kitchin was unhurt.

Over the Summer months a few of us had been keeping an eye on the new and fast growing sport of microlights. The microlight is a variation of the powered hang glider except that the pilot sits in a seat and wheels, instead of the pilot's legs, are used as the undercarriage. The engine and pusher prop is positioned above and behind the pilot's position. This sport was growing fast in the US and UK because of its safe low speed characteristics, ease of transport and low running costs and it held the promise of bringing sport aviation within reach of all.

It was decided to form an association in Ireland to cater for this growing sport and I agreed to act as secretary to get things moving. Terry Rowan, Tom Hudson, Paddy Byrne and Colm O'Rourke were among the founder members. The Irish Microlight Aircraft Association affiliated to the IAC in June 1980 and British Airways agreed to sponsor the first microlight to arrive in Ireland. It was flown by IAC president Tom Hudson who had for many years flown hang gliders. The microlight Skytrike was developed in England and had a thirty five foot wingspan, a foot operated throttle (the McPotty clothespeg design never caught on) and was powered by a 160 cc. engine. The prototype Skytrike turned out to be very underpowered and had to be flown with care particularly in turbulent conditions.

The Eagle was another microlight type on show at Fairyhouse, from UK dealer Brian Harrison. It was an American designed flex wing canard. Control was by handlebars which actuated tip draggers for banking while the canard elevator was linked to the position of the pilot's seat. The power unit consisted of twin Chrysler chain saw engines driving a single propeller. The throttle was operated by a lever fitted to the right hand handlebar not unlike the brake lever on a bicycle. Flying it was simple. Ask one of your helpers to start the engine. Point into wind. Pull in the throttle lever and when the airspeed reaches about thirty push the handlebars away from you. The ground recedes rapidly. Pull in the handlebars and settle down to level if noisy flight. Great fun. However the early engines were a teeny bit put out at having to operate at full throttle for long periods. This was of course completely understandable as they had been designed to power the intermittent operation of chainsaws. Occasionally they would stop. The unexpected beauty of silent flight was quickly drowned by the sound of an adrenalin powered heartbeat as the head scanned the ground for an immediate landing site. If only those early microlight seats could talk. Inflight restarting had not yet been invented.

This was the machine I had a share in with my husband Colm, Tom Hudson, Terry Rowan and Paddy Byrne. We couldn't wait to see it fly. The weather was not suitable however so the Eagle remained on static display for the show. We had to wait until the following weekend before the conditions were calm enough for safe flight. A few of the group flew it off Sandymount strand, Dublin on Saturday and the promenade walkers had much to entertain them. As the machine was a single seater your first flight was your first solo flight. It was both thrilling and scary at the same time and was most unlike the Cessna 150 which I was used to flying. After a short straight ahead hop I was very glad to be back on the sand again. Colm finished the day's flying with a wingtip into the sand landing which was too much for the delicate undercarriage to take. It collapsed. As the pilot's cloth seat was only a few inches off the ground it isn't too difficult to imagine what happened next. Quite right and nobody's behind is designed to withstand the shock of landing on the sand at 20 mph. The Eagle was repaired and back in action the next day but it was three months before Colm could sit down comfortably for any length of time. Thankfully the design of the microlight aircraft was to be much modified over the years. Today's examples are sturdy with powerful custom designed engines which can be re-started in flight and two seater machines are available for training.

The committee line-up for 1981 was more or less the same as for the 1980 display. Tom Hudson was chairman and display director. Terry Rowan, IAC president, looked after communications and security and Paddy Byrne was in charge of ground services. I was again acting as show co-ordinator. Mike Kelly was persuaded to do the commentary and Liam Byrne who had just published his own book, *History of Aviation in Ireland*, assisted him with his bulging files of facts and figures. British Airways was the sponsor and the date was Sunday 16 August at Fairyhouse. As a true spectacle of variety Air Spectacular '81 was hard to beat. Family admission was five pounds per car, and the weather was perfect. There was something for everybody as the various aerial acts demonstrated all aspects of sport aviation. The car parking was most disciplined as it was controlled by the army military police. The redcaps ensured that all the cars moved smoothly into the parking areas. Pleasure flights were very popular and the Aer Arran Islander and Irish Helicopters Bell Jet Ranger four seater helicopter were working hard to satisfy all their customers.

Arthur Wignall (see showmen) had just bought a Pitts Special 2A high performance aerobatic biplane from America. He opened the show at 14.30 hrs. and what a most exciting opening it was. He had intended to cut a ribbon stretched between two twenty foot high plastic poles using his wingtip in a knife edge attitude. On the first attempt he just missed it and went on to do another circuit of the track to set himself up for a second attempt. As he was doing this one of the plastic poles broke a few feet from its base and the other side was lowered to compensate. Arthur knew nothing about this as he set up for his second run. The ribbon was now five feet lower. Arthur knife edged his way down the display axis, reached the poles and cut the ribbon. The crowd loved it and we breathed a sigh of relief.

The Harvard finally made it this year. It was painted in Royal Canadian Air Force yellow and carried the registration G-BGPB. It was flown by Ray Pullan who was an ex RAF pilot now flying with British Airways. The Harvard did graceful loops and rolls while its 550 hp. Pratt and Whitney nine cylinder radial engine emitted its distinctive rasp. After displaying it departed for Jurby, Isle of Man, for another performance. We were sharing the costs of the Harvard with the IOM and co-operated with them in sharing acts many times over the years. We tried whenever possible to make sure that our show dates coincided.

The Model Aircraft Council of Ireland displayed its full range of control line and radio control aircraft. The high point for the youngsters was the toffee bomber which released one pound of delicious sweets suspended under streamers for all to collect. One modeller became so engrossed in his flying "STOP" sign that he did not hear the controllers telling him to finish his display as a four engined CL44 was approaching the field. When the "STOP" sign finally landed Capt. Mike Green of Aer Turas was able to demonstrate the lumbering giant which was enroute from Luton with a cargo of two horses. No doubt at a speed of 200 mph. it was their fastest trip around a racecourse.

At the start of the show we got a call from the display organisers at the Coventry air display in England to say that the red Hunter jet scheduled to appear at Fairyhouse at 15.47 hrs. had run off the runway, had burst a tyre and would not be able to make it. Panic. What was going to fill the ten minute gap this left in the tightly controlled programme. A quick call to Weston enlisted the willing help of Capt. Darby Kennedy and his flying school. At the appointed time a formation of his school aircraft lined up over the display axis for the start of their flypast.

In the general enclosure the vast trailer which accommodated the mock-up of a cabin and cockpit of the new Boeing 757 which would soon come into service on the British Airways Dublin-London route was on view. Parents and children queued patiently outside the aircraft and over 3,000 passed through the unit during the afternoon. The Air Corps also put on a very interesting static exhibition, while in the air the Fouga Magister jet display team led by Capt. Geoff White performed formation manoeuvres.

The two Gazelle helicopters were flown by Comdt. Ken Byrne, O/C helicopter squadron and Capt. Frank Condon. The Alouette helicopters 213 and 214 were not to be outdone and gave a colourful rescue demonstration using orange smoke to mark the rescue site.

Brian Lecomber displayed the Dunlop Pitts G-BOOK with aggressive brilliance before departing for another display at Farranfore, Co. Kerry. Air Spectacular '81 ended with a Microlight demonstration (the first in Ireland) and a colourful assembly of hot air balloons led by the giant special shape "Mr. Peanut" G-PNUT. The British Airways 56,000 cu. ft. Cameron built balloon G-BEND also flew. The Dublin Balloon Club's balloon piloted by David Hooper carried hang glider pilot Maxi McManus and his high performance Atlas hang glider to 3,000 ft. before setting up a rate of descent of 600 ft. per minute to allow the sail of the hang glider to fill sufficiently before release. When the rope was cut the hang glider dived to attain speed to give it the necessary lift for controlled flight. Not for the faint-hearted. The balloon pilot had his own problems. After releasing so much weight it took a lot of skill to arrest the ascent, stabilise the balloon and land before entering the Dublin ATC restricted area. The

53 Brian Lecomber displays the Dunlop Pitts

54 Mr Peanut

Irish Times balloon which had just completed a seventeen day tour of Ireland was flown by barrister Kevin Haugh who dropped off parachutist Neil Duiginn while climbing to 3,000 ft. This renewed the association between parachuting and ballooning which began in the last century when the earliest parachute jumps used the balloon basket as a launching platform.

Liam McCobb and Peter Hynes had their hands full keeping a close watch on all the aircraft during the afternoon's programme especially the private aircraft that had arrived on the field during the morning. They had not only to co-ordinate the aircraft taking part in the display, but also eliminate conflict with commercial and private aircraft operating out of nearby Dublin airport. This required constant communication with Dublin ATC using both radio and telephone. The field recorded over four hundred traffic movements during the afternoon and all were controlled from a five foot by seven foot open top starter's box on the far side of the finishing straight. Its elevated position gave a good view of the track and cut out distractions from the ground. Access to the box was by one set of steps so any unwanted boarders could easily be repelled. The borrowed radio equipment was powered by car batteries and the whole lot was kept working by our Mr. Fixit, David Gordon, an engineer with Aer Lingus. Telephones were mounted on upturned crates and headphones were essential to cut out the noise particularly when helicopters or jets were operating nearby. A tarpaulin folded in the corner of the starter's box was ready for use in case of rain. Pretty rough working conditions but the compensation was that you got to see the action first hand. The performers used the box as their reference point on the display axis. There was a great atmosphere in the box and when the show was in full swing the buzz was electric. The five people essential to the show's operation were beside one another and decisions could be made instantly.

Air Spectacular '81 brought to an end the three year contract with British Airways. The British Airways office in Dublin did not have the staff to cope with the added workload that Air Spectacular was creating as it grew larger each year. British Airways and the IAC were satisfied with the partnership which had enabled the show to establish itself on a secure footing for the future. The attendance had increased from 9,000 to 30,000 during the three years.

4
Enter Aer Rianta

55 *Aer Rianta logo*

Aer Rianta, the Irish Airports Authority, which had close links with the Irish Aviation Council for many years, was the obvious company for the IAC to approach about sponsorship to continue building Air Spectacular into international air display status. Aer Rianta had assisted over the previous Air Spectaculars by giving extra fire cover and by waiving landing and parking charges at its airports for display aircraft taking part in the show.

In early January 1982 the president of the IAC Terry Rowan contacted Gerry Harvey, assistant chief executive and a formal meeting was set up with Aer Rianta. The outcome was that Aer Rianta agreed to sponsor Air Spectacular '82. As this would be its first venture into the sponsorship arena Aer Rianta would review its commitment at the end of that year. Aer Rianta and its new chief executive Martin Dully saw the opportunity to promote itself and its services, particularly its duty free shops, to the public. By sponsoring this annual showcase at Fairyhouse it would also be assisting the promotion of sport and general aviation in a very positive way.

One of the first requirements was to change the date of the show to later in the month of August. The new date was 22 August. The original choice, the 15th, was clashing with a number of other events including the Carrolls Open golf championship which could possibly take from the gate. Aer Rianta appointed a permanent representative to our display organising committee so we welcomed Oliver McCann from public relations to the team. Oliver had been to see Air Spectacular '81 with assistant chief executive, Dublin Airport, Tom Cullen and was most impressed. From that moment he was sold on the magic of air displays which provided a fun-filled family day out with so many contrasting aspects of aviation. His favourite memory of '81 was the gathering of hot air balloons flying off into the late evening sun.

From the start we had been seeking permission from the Department

97

of External Affairs to allow foreign military aircraft to display at Air Spectacular. Such participation is common with other displays all over the world. This would add a terrific international dimension to our programme. 1982 was the breakthrough. Air Spectacular '82 was the year of the jets and featured the first foreign military jet aircraft to display at an Irish airshow since the Martin Baker Meteor jet appeared at Weston in the 1950s. An invitation was extended to the USAF. We received a favourable reply. The USAF would participate and we would be informed of the types of aircraft coming at a date nearer the show. In fact we were really not sure what was coming until we saw the aircraft flying over the display axis. What a sight that was. We were indebted to the US military attache in Dublin, Col. David Thompson, who smoothed the way for us. Summer '82 also saw the launching of the Miss Air Spectacular contest heats at Tamango's nightclub, Portmarnock, Co. Dublin. The object was to find the lovely lady who would win a free holiday and the title Miss Air Spectacular for the day.

Every year brought new schemes enabling the touts to make money at our and the public's expense. Once someone posed as an official collector at the base of the stands and charged £2 to adults and £1 to children for seats. He issued blue stickers to the unsuspecting public. Unfortunately he had scarpered before our security got wind of what was happening and checked it out. To solve that one we would make regular announcements that the only charge on the day was admission to the car park. Main stands were included.

We organised more static exhibits for the public, ATC Dublin and Met displays, Aer Rianta police dog display and aeroplanes on static. The Irish Aviation Museum mounted a most interesting exhibition of artifacts of our aviation heritage. Dick Killen of the museum showed the public around the collection.

Air Spectacular '82 with our new sponsor Aer Rianta was also special for the Irish Air Corps who were celebrating sixty years. There was a packed programme in store for the crowd of over 40,000 who jammed the roads by bus and car to get into Fairyhouse "international airfield" for that memorable day, Sunday 22 August. The admission charge was £5 per car load; without any doubt the bargain of the year. The showery blustery conditions meant problems with some of the acts but not for the public. Large traffic jams were reported on the surrounding roads by lunchtime. The USAF HH-55 Super Jolly Green Giant is a combat rescue helicopter which is normally based at Woodbridge, England. It is capable of carrying up to thirty eight troops in its hold and caused a stir among the early arrivals when it provided an impromptu display down the course before positioning on static on the crowd side of the track. Once safely

56 The US Air Force Jolly Green Giant

shut down the crew of airmen and women started a brisk trade selling
their 67th Aerosearch Rescue and Recovery Squadron patches and decals.
Earlier, and in true Cobham style, the HH-55, piloted by Capt. Bobdube
and with ATC man Gerry McCauley aboard, had flown over Dublin city
and the better known tourist sights around Ireland. Gerry was impressed
by the splendid views from this adjustable platform. He declares it the
only way to see Ireland. At lunchtime the Jolly departed to collect the
Aer Rianta board from Dublin Airport and bring them back to the VIP
reception at Fairyhouse.

The show opened with a brilliant aerobatic display from the two Pitts
Specials sponsored by Rothmans and flown by Marcus Edwards and
Dublin born John McClean. The team was called "Vixen Two". The
gasps and applause from the crowd carried to our side of the track as
necks craned skywards to see what was next. My favourite manoeuvre
was the mirror formation where John flew in mirror image upside down
a few feet above Marcus's top wing. When they had finished we dispatched
them quickly to Farranfore, Co. Kerry, where another air display was in
progress and they closed that show. At rehearsal the day before, Vixen

Two had taken up show commentator Mike Kelly and Colm O'Rourke
for some loops and spins. They each have a certificate to prove it, signed
by the pilot, and indicating the number of G's experienced during the
flight. Mike's commentary for the Vixen Two slot reflected the experiences
of his thirty minute flight. Both commented on Marcus' and John's skilful flying. Mike remembers that at one point the aircraft were so close
that though sitting in Marcus' Pitts he could read the instruments in John's
aircraft.

The Shorts 330 EI-BLP, a thirty seat commuter aircraft operated by
Avair on its internal air routes, did a series of flypasts with chief pilot
Capt. Henk Van Der Zee. At 15.00 hrs. an expectant hush settled on the
crowd as the Air Corps mounted a sparkling sixtieth birthday display with
aircraft from all squadrons taking part. The Puma, an all weather search,
rescue and troop carrying helicopter, on lease to the Air Corps, made its
debut for the Irish public, leading the formation of Alouette and Gazelle
helicopters. The Puma had already become a media star while dropping
supplies to those cut off during the heavy snow of the previous arctic
Winter. The Fouga Magister jets gave a precision display of wingtip-to-
wingtip formation flying and ended with a well co-ordinated crossover, Red
Arrows style. The Air Corps then showed off the maritime equipped Beechcraft King Airs used on fishery protection around the Irish coastline.

British Airways continued its association with Air Spectacular by sponsoring Wing Commander Wallis and his James Bond autogyro which was
appearing for the first time at Fairyhouse. Called "Little Nellie" it was
equipped with guns firing blanks and did battle with two Spectre agents
stupid enough to drive onto the course and take pot shots at the airborne
autogyro. The agents, alias Ronan Power of British Airways and Paddy
Byrne of the IAC, put up a good fight before fleeing in confusion from a
car belching flames and thick black smoke. The fire tender was quickly
on the scene. Getting the old banger to take part in this set piece was a
story in itself. Tom Kellett had persuaded Grange Motors to part with an
unroadworthy green Morris Oxford estate for use on the day. All that was
required was that it move briefly of its own volition for the battle sequence.
Some days before the show the garage towed the car to Fairyhouse. On
Saturday night Paddy Byrne checked the car, lifted the bonnet and to his
horror discovered that the battery, carburettor and radiator had disappeared. Early on Sunday morning Paddy scoured the local scrapyards
for replacement parts. Back on the field other problems screamed for
attention and the car was forgotten until out of the crowd appeared two
members of the Microlight fraternity, Liam Maddock and John Green from
Carlow, who could work magic with all things mechanical. Both had
designed and built their own Microlight aircraft. Up went the bonnet.

57 Air Corps Fouga Magister Jets

The Carlow men dived into the engine area assisted by Paddy's brother Noel. Three pairs of hands bypassed the radiator, borrowed a battery and by 15.00 hrs. the car burst into life. Wallis was then able to wire up the car with small explosive charges and it rolled on stage without ado.

Twelve months late the all red Hunter, which had run off the runway at Coventry and missed Air Spectacular '81, finally made it to Fairyhouse. G-HUNT was the only supersonic single seat jet in civilian ownership in Europe at that time and ex RAF pilot Adrian Gjertsen started his display with a run down the field at 500 knots before performing a most remarkable series of high speed jet aerobatics. This Hunter was similar to Neville Duke's all red Hunter prototype in which he took the world speed record to 727.6 mph. on 7 September 1953.

Joss Yates continued his involvement with Irish airshows when as Irish agent for British Aerospace he brought over the twin engined HS 748 demonstrator. This multi-role turboprop was displaying in its para dropping role with a capability of releasing up to forty eight paratroops from its wide rear cargo door. Thirty five members of the Parachute Club braved the blustery conditions to make the jump. A couple of parachutists had exciting landings including Tipperary girl Niamh O'Regan who tangled with a wooden rail on the side of the track before standing up unhurt to take a well deserved bow. The pilot then brought the 748 down to grass top height along the runway before heading back to Dublin Airport. A fine display.

At 16.00 hrs. the first of the USAF jets came roaring past. This was a Phantom, making history as the first of its type to appear in Irish skies. The noise was terrific as it echoed off the stands and left the spectators wide eyed and open mouthed. Just before the second wave of jets arrived we slipped in Anthony Hutton who flew G-AYAK, a high performance trainer used by the Russian air force and very rarely seen in the West. Appropriately this YAK carried a large red star on its fuselage. G-AYAK had been flown from behind the iron curtain by a defecting pilot some years previously. After his display Anthony departed for Dublin Airport to refuel before returning to England. He had reached the holding pattern over Dublin when out of the gloom appeared two USAF F-111s on a wide turn out from Fairyhouse. One F-111 pilot remarked to the other, "just missed my chance to hose a YAK."

In the "jolly green giant" helicopter on the ground at Fairyhouse Gerry McCauley ATC operated the UHF set and maintained contact with the USAF jets as they continued their display. The darkening cloud from a passing shower accentuated the vivid flame from their afterburners. On the final pass the moisture condensed into a visible shock wave as they pulled up into the low overcast and out over the Irish Sea heading back to their base in Lakenheath, England. America's most advanced fighter aircraft, the four F-15 Eagles from the 36th Tactical Fighter wing in Germany, lined up on the display axis from the southern end of the field and held in tight formation as they roared by. Some onlookers were caught unawares by the apparent quiet of these machines and removed their hands from their ears forgetting that the sound was following behind the

58 RF-4C
Phantom

59 USAF F-15 Eagles

60 British Aerospace 748

aircraft. When the sound wave hit, both stand and crowd shook with the tremendous vibration. After their final run, in line astern formation, the F-15s pulled up with vortices streaming from the wingtips into a vertical climb reaching 20,000 ft. in a couple of seconds. There was a welcome blue patch of sky at the time and we could see the F-15s level off beneath an overflying MEA 707 at 23,000 ft. They then rendezvoused with a tanker aircraft over the Irish Sea to re-fuel before routing to their base in Bitburg, Germany. The packed stands resounded to sustained applause for this final contribution from the men of the USAF. This was the first time that four F-15s had appeared together at an air display anywhere in Europe. One spares a thought for the bemused Middle East Airlines 707 pilot who watched the F-15s zooming up towards him and reported to Dublin ATC that he was about to be attacked!

Capt. Arthur Wignall, flying his first season in the Pitts Special for his new sponsor Harp, was on final pre-display checks at the holding point when the F-15s roared by. For a second he thought the Pitts had exploded. Arthur ended the show with some fine knife edge flying and aerobatics and concluded by jumping the fences with somewhat superior horsepower to the usual incumbents.

The picketing of the Fairyhouse gates by members of the Irish campaign for nuclear disarmament for thirty minutes before the show was generally good natured with the demonstrators showing great interest in the flying display. Our only real problem in the general enclosure was the abundance of unlicensed hawkers poaching business from the traders who had bought the sole concession rights for the day at Fairyhouse. Car boots were laden with cartons of chocolates, soft drinks and fruit. Trestle tables were erected and dismantled in minutes only to pop up elsewhere. Paddy Byrne had his hands full controlling these resourceful operators in his own firm but polite way.

Course manager Norman Colfer calmly held fort in the general enclosure fielding the public's queries at the secretary's office. A gentleman to deal with, he was a great supporter of the show and enjoyed the novelty of these mad aviators who invaded his racecourse once a year. The Jolly departed Fairyhouse carrying the Aer Rianta board of directors back to Dublin Airport and bringing to a close an historic Air Spectacular to be remembered as the year the jets came. The public response to the USAF appearance was terrific. The question was what could we now do to top that? Our audience was steadily becoming more sophisticated. What could we pull out of the hat for 1983? We had twelve months to work on it. Our sponsor Aer Rianta was pleased with its first experience and felt we had done a good job. They decided to renew the sponsorship for the following year.

61 The all red Hunter, G-Hunt

Air Spectacular '83 was held on Sunday 21 August, again at Fairyhouse. To get the public to arrive earlier in the morning and avoid the massive traffic jams around lunchtime we opened a two-tier admission of £5 per car before twelve noon and £6 thereafter. Forty five thousand people made their way to Fairyhouse equipped with ear muffs, binoculars, cameras as well as campchairs and picnics for the day's entertainment. To occupy the extra crowd during the morning we expanded the entertainment schedule before the main show. The Hot City orchestra was booked to provide live music. Ian Dempsey, RTE DJ, had a mobile studio to cater for the pop fans. The Irish Aviation Museum mounted a fine display of engines, models and photographs. Video and film shows were available and the Society of Amateur Aircraft Constructors, thanks to the help of chairman Mick Donoghue, set up a most popular IBM computer flight simulation where spectators could test their skills. Johnny Carroll and his team from MACI mounted an interesting display of model aircraft flying for the early birds.

The weather had caused a lot of worry. On Saturday there was widespread fog and we had to cancel the planned afternoon rehearsal for the American A 10 jets. The only movement on the airfield was a formation of very low flying birds. There was a lot of praying that night despite a promising forecast. When I woke I consulted my favourite yardstick, the ESB power station's 600 ft. high twin chimneys at Poolebeg, one and a half miles from my house. I could see them clearly. I knew we were in business. Unfortunately one of the racecourse employees did not. He had panicked and telephoned the RTE newsroom to say the show might be cancelled. As I arrived at Fairyhouse pandemonium had set in. The lines were jammed. Were we in a go or a no-go situation? By 09.10 hrs. Fairyhouse was alive with committee members and PR people, directories in hand, telephoning to one and all that the show was definitely on. The weather took its time in exposing true blue and unfortunately the C 141 giant starlifter went by overhead unable to let down in the murk. Liam McCobb (ATC) got a glimpse of it at 2,000 ft. He was one of the few who did.

By noon the Jolly Green Giant helicopter was on its way from Dublin Airport which had just opened and Anthony Hutton reported that he was on his way from London in his Harvard. On arrival he mistook that part of the racecourse we used for parking aircraft as the active runway and plonked the Harvard down on unprepared and unchecked ground. One of his better landings he reported despite causing more than a little anxiety. Just before the show briefing I had a call from the pilot of the vintage Comper Swift, the only airworthy example of its type in the world. Part of the wooden and canvas aeroplane had been chewed up by the pro-peller of a taxi-ing Cessna on the ramp at Farranfore. The man was almost in tears. He had just spent three years restoring the Comper to flying status. Tom Hudson would have to re-write the programme once again.

Richard Goode flying the high performance Pace Spirit monoplane created quite a stir with a beautiful display. At the briefing Richard requested that a bucket of water be delivered to the aeroplane immediately after displaying. Despite general amusement it was duly dispatched to await the hero's return. Richard hopped out, grabbed the bucket and tossed the cold water over his very hot engine. This was done to force cool the engine before heading off to another display in England. He was fed up of his previous practice of handswinging the hot engine, and had hit on a simple solution — a dash of cold water.

Mike Kelly on commentary asked the crowd to look in the general direction of the sun to observe the aircraft approaching with parachutists. Quickly realising his mistake he corrected himself but the newspapers next morning wryly reported "Airshow commentator tries to blind the crowd." Mike would not make that mistake again. Seventeen parachutists were dispatched from the Shorts 330 described by one journalist as the biggest bread van in the world. They made a colourful sight spiralling down to a safe landing. During parachute display all propellers and rotors are stopped.This is pre-arranged at the display briefing. Tragic accidents have happened to parachutists worldwide where this rule has not been observed.

The Air Corps presented an exciting routine demonstrating once again to the taxpayers exactly what they were paying for. Each item showed the high degree of professionalism to which these men are trained in their flying careers. One novel item went down particularly well with the youngsters, an "it's a knockout" style race against the clock between

62 & 63 *Air Corps Alouette (above) and Gazelle (below) Helicopters*

two Alouette helicopters with winchmen dangling underneath. Without touching the ground the winchmen filled measured beakers with water fetched from a barrel on the far side of the field. The race was hard fought and demonstrated the superb skill of the Air Sea rescue service whose pilots flew the two machines. The two Gazelle helicopters were fitted with coloured smoke which highlighted their demonstration and they finished their display with a bow to the audience who responded with loud applause.

The Government executive HS 125 jet made its first public appearance at an Irish display with a flypast. One display I had looked forward to was the Spitfire G-FIRE. However, it arrived overhead late and had to cut short its display as the pilot was low on fuel and had to divert to Dublin Airport. Coming in at £1,250 it was the costliest three minutes we ever had to pay for. A formation of three USAF A 10s based at RAF Bentwaters had come over to Dublin Airport. Led by Capt. Kevin Barley they began their display of very tight turns and straffing passes which demonstrated the A 10's high manoeuvrability. All turns and figures of eight were completed within the confines of the racecourse. Its combat role is providing close support for the Army thus getting its nickname "tankbuster". When the aircraft arrived at Dublin Airport on Friday keen interest was shown in the weapons bays. What sophisticated firepower would they unfold? The onlookers were disappointed to discover no more than a bag of golf clubs, the most hazardous piece of equipment on board that weekend. In fact all military display aircraft are stripped of weapons and missiles and the bomb shaped objects carried underneath are in reality long range fuel tanks which greatly extend the operating range. During an average six minute display, an A 10 is estimated to use over £2,000 of fuel. After the A 10s, Paddy Robinson flying the Aer Arran Islander took to the air and what followed was the most amazing five minutes as he imitated the tight turns of the A 10s. Anything you can do!

Norrie Grove, Chief Pilot of Slingsby, demonstrated the state of the art single engined Firefly light military trainer at its first public demonstration outside the UK. This aircraft is built entirely from glass reinforced plastic. Norrie put it through a full aerobatic sequence doing eight point rolls, loops and stall turns. Vixen Two became three when John and Marcus were joined by Andy Wallbridge from Blackpool who had been an engineer and pilot for the Rothman's team reserve aircraft. They performed some very skilled formation flight and hair's breath opposition passes. Sadly this was to be John and Andy's last display at Fairyhouse. The three hour main display finished with a tribute to two hundred years of balloon flight with the Dublin Ballooning Club's Cameron 65 taking to the skies to be joined by the newest design, the one man Cloudhopper balloon sponsored by Smirnoff and piloted by Colin Prescot. The pilot sits in a harness on top of the propane cylinder which feeds the burner unit located above his head. The hot air from the burner is retained by the 17,000 cu. ft. silicon proofed polyester canopy. The sport has come a long way from man's first flight in France in 1783. We remembered in a special way the courage and vision of the two Mongolfier brothers, the paper manufacturers who started it all.

Runway incursion was a constant cause of concern during these shows, incursion by spectators and pilots alike. Some members of the public would stroll from the far end of the course having come through hedges on to the runway area. It was a constant headache keeping this most hazardous area clear. A woman blissfully unaware once crossed the runway pushing a baby in a buggy. Little did she realise the grave danger had the eagle eyed ATC controller not stopped the aircraft lining up for take-off below her and just out of her sight. Our security team rigidly enforced the use of a walkway beyond the runway and used hospitality cars to transport people to and from the display control. Terry Rowan and his team had the unenviable task of making all this work. The consequences of a breach of the security measures could not even be contemplated.

64 Smirnoff one man Balloon

Looking back, 1984 was one of those really bad years for aviation in Ireland. Arthur Wignall, aerobatic pilot extraordinary, was to die in Sligo in April while flying his Pitts at an aerobatic seminar. Richard Goode, who had displayed for us the previous year, cheated death but was badly injured when his Pace Spirit disintegrated and crashed in May. A month later John McClean, a skilled pilot and most pleasant person whom I got to know over the years, together with Andy Wallbridge were killed while flying near Blackpool. Good pilots, fine people, killed and injured doing what they enjoyed most of all. Little did we know when announcing our Air Spectacular line up a month before the display what disaster would strike at Fairyhouse. Every year we review and revise our accident and emergency plans most carefully. Air Display flying is not without hazard, neither is crossing the road or travelling by car to the display. Air Spectacular '84 was to feature a wide spectrum of aircraft, from the latest American jet fighter, the F-16, to the first hot air airship seen here. It would include a formation of powered gliders, air force participation from America and France and commercial items from Aer Lingus and Aer Turas. It promised to be the biggest and best show ever in Ireland.

In early August the second European precision flying championships came to Ireland. The championship director was Peter Costello. The precision flying committee was chaired by Tom Farrington and it was all under the auspices of the Irish Aviation Council. The competitive events such as navigation exercises and spot landings took place from 8 to 10 August with practice being allowed during the first two days. The venue was Casement aerodrome by kind permission of the Minister of Defence and station commander Lt. Col. John O'Brien who was the Department's representative on the council worked unstintingly to ensure that all went smoothly. There was an Irish team and seven other teams from Norway, Sweden, Switzerland, England, Yugoslavia and Finland together with the defending champions Poland led by their jovial team manager Jan Baran, a co-pilot with LOT, the Polish airline. The Polish were flying their 260 hp. Wilga aircraft. They proved once again that they were masters of precision flying by carrying off the top prize. In company with the team flying the Finnish air force Valmet they stayed on to take part in Air Spectacular on Sunday 12 August.

Air Display morning dawned with a grey sky, light winds and a fairly solid overcast at 1500 ft. Once again the flypast of the USAF transporter had to be scrubbed. The C-5A Galaxy could not let down through the murk and continued its flight to America. The light winds did allow Fairyhouse to see its first hot air airship. During the morning at the VIP reception there was a poignant moment when IAC president Brian Kearney presented the IAC's premier award, the Fitzmaurice Trophy, a posthumous tribute to Arthur Wignall. Arthur's mother had flown over from Southport to accept the award. She was to meet Joss Yates, Arthur's first employer in Ireland and to discover first hand why he was held in such high esteem by other pilots.

Good crowds were reported during the morning. The final figure was over 50,000. Once again we had many static attractions and the pleasure flight operators were busy. The model aircraft display during the morning featured Irish Helicopter's little brother and there was much interest as this beautiful radio controlled scale model, an exact copy of the original, was put through its paces. Up in the box we had at last acquired a perspex roof to repel passing showers. After '83 we had to insist on proper cover. During the heavy showers we had used a tarpaulin which worked fine until pools formed overhead and we were in danger of eventual flooding from the weight of water. We had to push the water off from time to time, much to the discomfort of the commentary team beneath us. Liam Byrne had one of those shocking experiences, potentially very dangerous, when he picked up a truly "live mike" and caught a substantial current of electricity. Like a true professional he finished his sentence before casting the offending mike to the ground. A few choice words were then hurled at the PA electrician and his peculiar notion of a live performance.

There was an international flavour to the display briefing. Apart from the Polish and Finnish pilots, American and French accents also enlivened the jockeys' weigh-in room. Martin Dully, chairman of Aer Rianta, declared the show open after which a lone Pitts commenced its take off run. Nobody deserved to open an airshow more than Marcus Edwards, the only surviving member of the "Vixen" formation team. He flew a beautiful seven minute routine which he dedicated to the memory of his team mates John and Andy. This was followed by Mick Donoghue's yellow VP1 homebuilt. The next act comprised a most unusual visiting homebuilt often called the "back to front" aeroplane because of its strange appearance. The Long Eze took its owner eighteen hundred hours to build over a year and a half. The all composite construction was powered by a Rolls Royce Continental engine of 130 hp. giving it a range of 2,000 nautical miles on forty two imperial gallons, almost 48 nm. per gal. which is more economical than many cars. Don Foreman had flown the aircraft from England the day before and had landed at Weston. Ronan Power of British Airways who sponsored Don's appearance at Air Spectacular went to meet him and was invited for a flight. Ronan had just recovered from an illness and was not feeling the best that morning. He asked him to take it easy, just a few gentle trips around the circuit at Weston would do nicely thank you. After two power dives and a final high speed climb to 1000 ft., Ronan was finished. On landing Don innocently asked Ronan "any chance of further sponsorship from British Airways?" The response is not recorded.

Mr. Harvard himself, Anthony Hutton, in preparation for the 1984 season had approached the owners of other Harvards in England with a view to getting a large formation of these rumbling vintage aircraft together for display work. Over the previous Winter, under the guidance of ex RAF Sqd. Ldr. Colin Dodds, they worked out an attractive routine with smoke for the four Harvards whose Pratt and Whitney radial engines give them their evocative rasping sound. Capt. Bill Howarth was in his element looking on: he had trained in one during his RAF days. "A real aeroplane" he said, "none of this tin can rubbish of nowadays." The four Harvards took off from Fairyhouse in pairs and made an impressive sight as they passed down the course in line astern before their final climb out and departure to another air display at Jurby on the Isle of Man. They never made that display having to fly above eighty miles of overcast. They landed at Ronaldsway on the other side of the island which had good conditions. Only a few miles away Jurby was in fog with two hundred meters visibility.

15.00 hrs. and the traditional display slot for the Irish Air Corps opened with a formation of three King Airs led by Comdt. Ralph James, the O/C Maritime Squadron since 1983. Two of the King Airs were in distinctive "day glo" stripes and are used on maritime patrols. The third King Air is used in a training and transport role. They were followed by a formation of three helicopters led by an Alouette III. 1984 was a special year for the Helicopter Squadron and marked twenty one years of helicopter operations with the Air Corps. During that time the Squadron had been responsible for saving 270 lives and had transported 1400 patients to hospital. Their motto which is incorporated in the Squadron crest is fitting: "that others may live". Capt. Harvey O'Keefe manoeuvred the Alouette and his winchman over the Air Corps yellow rapid intervention fire truck which had been hijacked by a masked bandit who was now standing on top as it moved down the runway. The winchman quickly accounted for the bandit before both were winched back into the helicopter. Capt. Paul Fry and Lt. Donal Cotter flying two Gazelle helicopters gave exciting runs from opposite sides of the field and featured close passovers before ending with a bow to the crowd. The highlight of the dramatic Air Corps display were the four Siai Marchetti Warriors which approached in formation from behind the grandstand. They finished with a solo Warrior attacking a target in the centre of the racecourse. Much pyrotechnics provided flashes and smoke before the solo Warrior departed giving us a victory roll. The Air Corps display finished with a single Fouga Magister flown by Lt. Dermot McCarthy which gave a fine demonstration of high speed jet aerobatics.

65 Harvard Formation Team

The general announcement over the public address of "all aircraft props on the ground stopped please" heralded the mass parachute drop by members of the Irish Sport Parachute Association from a Skyvan. Included in the jump were RTE personalities Angus McNally and Barry Lang, both skilled parachutists, who were dropping in aid of the National Association for Cerebral Palsy in a competition to see who would land nearest the target. The French Air Force Alpha jet flown by Lt. Bourlard based at Cazaux, France, became the first French military jet aircraft to display at an Irish air show. Starting from Dublin Airport the two seater trainer went through its eight minute performance and finished with a high speed pass.

In stark contrast the Fournier Duo flying two RF4 powered gliders, Brendan O'Brien and John Taylor, gave a ten minute display of graceful formation and synchronised aerobatics including the unique gliding inverted mirror where one glider formates upside down on top of the other. As the powered gliders are not fitted with an inverted fuel system the top glider flown by Brendan performs this manoeuvre in a true "power

66 *Powered Gliders in mirror formation, flown by Brendan O'Brien and John Taylor*

off" glide. Performed to music this elegant aerial ballet duo with their paths traced out in smoke was an oasis of peace. A quiet zone before the next provider of noise arrived. The ballet ended and the crowd was relaxed. Suddenly the two F-15 single seater Eagles from the USAF 32nd FTS based in Holland flashed by doing a fast run in with afterburners on before returning for a more sedate close formation slow pass.

The four seater basic trainer Valmet is a single engined low wing monoplane from Finland. It was flown by Finnish Air Force pilot Hannu Halonen who gave an enthralling display of the aircraft's impressive agility and robustness as he performed inverted loops, spins and rolls. We welcomed Aer Lingus back to display at Air Spectacular for the first time since 1978 as the Shorts 360 commuter flown by Captain Tom Croke was put through its paces demonstrating some high speed and approach configuration passes along the display axis. On its return to Dublin Airport it was back to work to operate a scheduled flight to Edinburgh. At 16.20 hrs. the three single engined 260 hp. high wing monoplane Wilgas from Poland led by Jan Baran who, together with his team mates Vitold Sviadek and Chris Lenartovicz, had successfully defended their European Precision Flying Championship title the previous week, took off to begin their dis-

67 Jan Barran leads the Wilgas formation

play. The following five minutes remain frozen in my memory. The three Wilgas commenced their display with a left hand circuit. Jan Baran was in the lead flying SP-AFX. On lining up from the northern end of the field the formation changed to line astern before starting the next run along the display axis. Baran who was now in the middle of the formation had overshot the display axis on the final turn. He was rejoining in a left hand turn at a height of approximately 300 ft. with forty four degrees of flap extended when suddenly his Wilga rolled rapidly to the left, the nose dropped and it descended almost vertically, rotating about one turn before hitting the ground near the aircraft parking area and on the line of the display axis very close to where the Harvards had been parked a few hours previously. Baran was killed instantly. The smoke rising from the wreckage signalled the saddest moment in the short history of Air Spectacular. In the control box I just could not believe what was happening. It was as if it had all taken place in slow motion. Once I saw the Wilga fall I knew that it was not going to recover in time. Then we were all galvanised into action. The fire tenders which were situated just below us reacted immediately and the Air Corps RIV and large foam tender crashed through the fence to reach the scene. This procedure had been agreed beforehand as the fence was of light wooden construction and breaking through would save valuable seconds. Terry Rowan and his security team arrived on the scene with hand held fire extinguishers between ten and twenty seconds after impact. Ian Ashpole the airship pilot also ran over with his extinguisher. The tenders were applying foam within sixty seconds of the accident. Brian Lecomber who had observed the crash from the cockpit of his Pitts some yards away said the response of the emergency services would have done credit to the biggest displays in England. Dr. Colm Killeen was in the medical centre in the general enclosure. He heard the crash and was out the door with Bernard Woods commandant of the Knights of Malta before he was called on the radio. He got to the scene in less than a minute. Unfortunately there was nothing that he or anybody else could do. Baran had been killed immediately on impact.

Mike Kelly who was on the public address microphone at the time prevented even further tragedy when he ordered everybody in a clear and forceful voice to "clear the runway". The dozens of people who were running on to the runway stopped in their tracks. Mike had saved them from certain injury as the two other Wilgas were coming in to land. He had a most positive influence on the spectators and prevented panic by remaining completely calm, unemotional and objective. Like the rest of us he was stunned into silence for a few moments but then knew he must take complete control or more accidents were likely to happen. For the remainder of the show he provided the spectators with information as it came to hand and worked hard to calm and reassure them.

At all the "what if" and accident briefings we had held, Mike often wondered how he would react in this very situation, the most frightening and shocking of airshow experiences, the fatal crash in front of the crowd. Air Spectacular '84 tested him as it tested all of us and we are amazed to this day how we managed to suppress our emotions and calmly continue with the task in hand. All the careful planning paid off. Dr. Colm Killeen took the two shocked surviving Polish team members back to the medical centre and the rescue teams led by Terry Rowan cleared the crash area of people and roped it off. In the accepted practice and tradition of air displays everywhere the show must go on. There are many reasons for such a seemingly heartless decision: one is simply to ensure that the exit routes are kept clear for ambulances and emergency services. We checked that the fire tender cover was still adequate and that the runway was totally clear. We were on automatic as Tom Hudson directed the F-111 to be called in for two flypasts demonstrating its swing wing configurations before it headed back to base in Upper Hayford. We were fortunate to have an aerobatic pilot of Brian Lecomber's calibre next. He gave the performance of his life and succeeded in distracting attention from events on the ground. It was one of the most impressive Pitts demonstrations I have seen. He left for Abbeyshrule immediately afterwards to close their display. It was only when he got to Abbeyshrule that the full impact of the tragedy hit him.

68 USAF "Swing-Wing" F-111

The F4 Phantom from RAF Alconbury came in low and as it drew closer the afterburners went on, the speed increased and the shock wave condensation flickered across the wings. After the low blustering beat up it pulled into a steep climb halfway along the course with its twin burners glowing against the grey overcast. The performance drew spontaneous applause. The Aer Turas CL44 flown by Capt. Nigel Budd and first officer Hugh Caulfield was an impressive sight as it flew low over the course. At the halfway point the CL44 was rolled into a steep bank to maintain a tight 360 degree turn around the airfield. On rolling out in front of the crowd the aircraft pulled up into a steep climb displaying remarkable agility for such a big machine.

The show officially ended after two hours and twenty two minutes with the USAF F-16 flown by Major Alain Kamerer from Hahn base in West Germany. This was the first of its type to be displayed to the Irish public and it performed wingovers and vertical climbs which demonstrated the aircraft's brute force and agility. Ian Ashpole flying Smirnoff Cloudship, the smallest pressurised airship ever built then took to the air with the appropriate registration G-WZZZ. He flew the airship up and down the display axis. In 1986 Ian was entered in the *Guinness Book of Records* for performing a trapeze act while suspended from a hot air balloon over England at a height of 16,420 ft.

When the display finished I slowly left the box and the enormity of the Wilga tragedy struck home. I wanted to pack up my equipment and go home. Bill Howarth took me aside and told me to get this into perspective. "There was nothing you or anybody else could do. It was between a pilot and his aeroplane". I was grateful to him. Brian Kearney came over just then and pushed me into a room where a small gathering had assembled for a drink. It was better to talk about it before going home. They were right of course and it did help to talk it out. The many letters and phone calls over the next few days with their wonderful words of support helped to ease the pain.

The two Polish pilots departed on the Tuesday following the body of their dead colleague on its sad journey to Warsaw. After taking off from Dublin Airport the two Wilgas headed over to Fairyhouse and dipped their wings in salute above the crash site before heading east and home. Tom Hudson was at Fairyhouse at the time. It was a very emotional moment. A few weeks later a letter was received from the president of the Polish Aero Club, Brig. Gen. Hermaszewski, expressing grateful thanks for the friendship and assistance received by the team after the crash. As a token of appreciation he generously offered the use of their aircraft to the Irish Precision Flying Team for the 1986 European Precision Flying Championships which would be held in Poland.

My enthusiasm for another air show faded a bit over the following months. It was not helped when an Irish Sunday newspaper the following weekend reported on the accident and published three colour photographs of the wreckage with the pilot still inside. They were taken a few moments after the crash. To say it was in bad taste would be putting it very mildly. This newspaper, which is read by families on Sunday, splashed all the gory details of the pilot's very public death across its inner pages.

Some officials from the Department of Communications were among the spectators at the display and they began a preliminary investigation into the accident very shortly afterwards. At no time was the public at Fairyhouse in any danger. The rules and regulations concerning air displays are there to protect them. These regulations did not extend to the people who were in a field overlooking the runway right underneath the display axis and those on the runway approach at the northern end. Someone was trying to make a few pounds but without proper concern for the safety of those he was admitting. Stewards tried to warn those people of the danger of their situation but unfortunately the field was outside our jurisdiction.

In early February the IAC received a letter from Aer Rianta asking the board to consider holding Air Spectacular '85 at Cork airport to tie in with Cork's 800 years festivities. The display would be Cork airport's contribution to the octocentennial celebrations. After some contact with our affiliated groups in the area which brought an enthusiastic response and the promised co-operation of management and staff at the airport led by general manager Barry Roach, we felt that we would be able to meet the challenge. Over the following weeks many trips were made to Cork to plan the event on the ground. Tom Hudson was busy ensuring that the ongoing planning between the local committees and the IAC was interfacing smoothly. Meanwhile I was back on the treadmill of seeing what was available in the flying world for Sunday 18 August 1985. In May the welcome news came through that the crack Italian Air Force jet formation team the "Frecce Tricolori" the tricoloured arrows, would be joining us at Cork. This was a great boost. For the first time we had access to a real airport. We could really broaden the show. All of the display acts could land at the field and most would be available for static display to the public. Top facilities would be available for the aircraft on the ground. In order to set up an area for displaying static aircraft one of the runways had to be closed. The shorter east/west one was selected and crowd barriers were set up at the runway edge so the public could see what was happening on the ground as well as in the air. Toilets, tents, power, water and a host of other conveniences all had to be planned for and laid on.

The local flying groups and model aircraft clubs gave tremendous support led enthusiastically by Nuala O'Donoghue, Jim Clifford and Richard Murphy. By early August we had a packed programme ready for the special Cork Air Spectacular. As well as the nine MB 339s of the Frecce Tricolori there would be two F-104s of the German maritime corps Viking display team. The French would be bringing two Alpha jets and the Americans would display an F-15, F-111 and F-16 as well as putting the HH53 Jolly Green Giant helicopter on static display. The Irish Air Corps were planning a twenty minute display. Richard Goode who had made a good recovery from his injuries was leading the civilian input. A powered gliding formation team was booked as was Wing Commander Wallis and "Little Nellie", out to see if there was a "Spectre" branch in Cork. Sally B and the Harvard formation would be there and also contributions from our own affiliated groups. The three hour show would span the entire flight experience. RTE announced that the station would record a thirty minute television documentary on the show to be hosted by Pat Kenny and broadcast on the evening. It would provide a flavour of the event to the thousands of people who would not be able to travel to Cork for the day and we were delighted. We expected a lot of our usual following to make the journey by bus and car and on the SAAC special train which was the brainchild of SAAC president Tony Murphy. He had the idea of hiring a train and offering the Dubs an all-in package of train, bus to show and admission ticket as a good way to make funds for SAAC. He offered to take the risk of the venture himself. Booking at the start was slow and there was apprehension in the Murphy household but by the weekend of the show the train was fully booked and people were telephoning his home at all hours looking for a ticket at any price. Air Spectacular had caught the imagination of people from all corners of the country.

The organising team moved down to Cork at the start of that weekend. I took the caravan so that I could be on site at all times. The Italians arrived on Friday evening in their eleven colourful MB 339s. The aircraft made a splendid and distinctive sight parked on the ramp together with their twin engined transport, the G-222 carrying the spares and team baggage. Saturday was hectic setting up our equipment. The control centre was located in a rented Portakabin. The final crowd barriers had been set in place and Paddy was busy with the public address system in the general enclosure where the last marquees were being erected. On Saturday night there was a terrific turnout from local volunteers for steward duty and a million other tasks. The final briefing of ground teams was held in the airport fire station as the rain came down in torrents outside. The weather was causing real concern at this stage. The airport had been closed for most of the day due to fog but we hoped for the best. Shortly after the briefing I was called to the control centre. Richard Goode was reported overdue and flying somewhere in the south east of Ireland trying to get to Cork. ATC had contacted other airfields where he might have landed but there were no reports. We were very worried. Where had he got to? The poor visibility with all that high ground around him flying a Pitts Special which has very basic instruments added up to hazardous circumstances. Finally a message came through. He had landed safely in a field and we had a telephone number for his hotel. A very tired Richard answered me to relate his attempts to find Cork airport in the worst weather he had ever met in his entire flying career. He had set off from Belfast after their display late on Saturday afternoon. Dublin was reporting sunny weather and visibility over thirty miles. He headed south without getting further weather forecasts, an action he admitted was foolish and dangerous and nearly cost him his life. The weather closed in as he approached Cork and the cloud base got steadily lower and lower. He was finally trapped in the Blackwater valley near Fermoy, some forty miles north of Cork city. With clouds on the hills on either side he had no option but to follow the river down to the sea at Youghal. He was so low that at one point he flew underneath a line of power cables stretching across the river. This terrified him. Worse was to come. When he reached the coast there was a shifting layer of sea fog rising to meet the low cloud. He realised then that he could not possibly reach Cork airport which is 500 ft. above sea level and would be totally fog bound. He decided to try for Waterford by creeping along the coast. The cloud base was still dropping, fuel was getting low, darkness was setting in and the rain was pouring down. On the verge of panic he was understandably short of ideas. He would have to land even though the average field in his area was no more than eighty yards long with stone walls at either end. He could see three fields ahead no more. He picked one that looked a possibility but felt sure he would hit the boundary wall. Damage to the Pitts yes but at least he might walk away from it. With less than ten minutes of fuel remaining it seemed his only option. As he started his approach he saw a slightly longer field, the only one for miles around he discovered later, and dropped the Pitts in hard. Breaking action on the wet grass was negligible. The Pitts seemed to roll on forever, the wall came closer and looked more solid by the second. His heart pounded and his body willed the aircraft to stop. It did, twenty yards from the wall. The pounding in his head was noisier than the rain on the canopy. A local farmer was soon on the spot and Richard was installed in Lawler's Hotel in Dungarvan.

With much relief I retired that night to a rather damp caravan. The mist swirled around outside and I had a sinking feeling about weather prospects for next day. By 09.30 on Sunday the met office advised us that the fog was not going to lift and the cloudbase would remain below 200 ft. for the day. There was no option but to cancel. A year's work down the drain. The acts were in place, the stage was set but the curtain of fog refused to lift. Convoys were already on the way to Cork. The catering lorries and the Funfair were on the road from Dublin in glorious sunshine as was the cavalcade of our loyal supporters.

Heavy traffic was reported on all roads into Cork city. A fire engine was dispatched to a vantage point some distance from the airport to block off the road and advise people that the show had been cancelled. As soon as the decision was made announcements were broadcast on local and national radio and on TV news headlines.

The special train which had left Dublin at 08.20 hrs. was stopped at Charleville and Tony Murphy announced to the hushed groups that the show had been cancelled. For an instant they thought he was joking. After all they were looking out at sunshine. Then there was general agreement that they should press on to Cork anyway and make the best of the day. CIE laid on coaches at the station to meet them and had two tours planned, one to Fota Wild Life Park and the other to the site of the moving statue at Ballinspittle shrine. People got to see parts of Cork they would not normally have visited. Getting back on the train that evening they were in good spirits. One satisfied customer asked Tony to be sure to contact him if he was laying on anything like this again. It was a great relief.

The met office was right. The fog did not lift. The irony was that Fairyhouse was bathed in sunshine all day.

Once the decision to cancel had been made I rushed to the nearest phone, files in hand, to cancel acts that might not yet have started on their way to Cork. It was a desperate if modest attempt to mitigate the massive financial loss we were about to incur. The tragic crash at Air Spectacular '84 had been my lowest ebb. This cancellation although of course quite different was a deep disappointment. It was the terrible waste of a year's work with nothing to show for it. I felt sorry for the rest of the team and especially the local committees who had been so enthusiastic about having the show at "Cork 800". A good airshow is the fitting reward for such dedicated voluntary labour and this was denied by the weather. My heart also went out to people like Richard Goode who had tried so hard to make it, to Ken Wallis who had trailed "Little Nellie" from Norfolk to share the mist with us and to the Italian Frecce Tricolori jet aerobatic team. What a superb show they would have given us. It was the first time in eighteen years they had to cancel due to weather. The Irish Air Corps were there in force ready to give a sparkling performance. The German Vikings waiting at Shannon airport had to make do with a tour of Kerry and Clare in place of showing Cork their Starfighters on

69 Italian Aerobatic Team, Frecce Tricolori

70 Low cloud at Cork

123

the Sunday. The USAF F-15 and F-16s gave an impromptu display at Shannon and during one run the ATC controllers in the tower were actually looking down on the jets as they flashed past. Performers like to entertain crowds. The applause and the feedback is their main reason for doing it. The fog at Cork cheated them. It cheated all of us.

The IAC had invested over £30,000 to bring Air Spectacular to Cork and with no gate receipts it faced a huge loss. On Sunday evening the low cloud was still there and rain was falling. A very sombre group was working off its frustrations, dismantling over seven hundred metal crash barriers and loading them on to trailers ready for the journey back to Dublin. Brian Kearney, IAC president and his wife Dara, Tom Hudson and Jennifer, Paddy Byrne, his son Alan and friend Ray and Colm and myself. We tried to cheer each other up but in reality we were a sorry mob and the rain made it seem worse. In all the gloom and doom the Aer Rianta runway patrol took pity on us and appeared out of the mist in his van with a load of hot dogs and cans of soft drinks. It made the world seem a slightly better place, a kind gesture and very welcome. We talked about all the good shows as we worked and we had some great memories to share. Now we were sampling the bad times. As we struggled in the rain heaving those heavy metal barriers one thing became very obvious. When things are going well one is surrounded by the freeloaders, hangers on and hot air merchants, always so quick to tell one how it should be done. Where are they now we asked ourselves? A little sorry for ourselves perhaps, well who could blame us?

71 Cork 800 logo

5
View from the Ground

The organisation of the following year's Air Spectacular begins at the final wrap up meeting of the current show at which all the lessons learned are pondered upon, brickbats and bouquets dispensed and the committee of victims for the next year's show are selected. At the end of every Air Spectacular most of us say "that's enough, not worth the pressure". That's how you feel immediately after the show. It is a combination of elation at the success of the display but also exhaustion from the effort it took to get it right.

It takes a little time for the situation to come into proper perspective again and for the enthusiasm to bubble once more. I now realise that one particular year we made a bad mistake by holding this final wrap up meeting only a few days after the show when feelings were still running a wee bit high. Things were said that with a few more days cooling off would not have been so pointed or so hard hitting. It was indeed the night of the long knives. This of course happens with the best committees when all are working under such pressure and responsibility while trying to do their best in the situation presented on the day.

In fact the team spirit generated within the committee is a very potent force. We are driven by the love of aviation and the challenge of making it work by presenting an organised and professionally run display. This force sees us through the hiccups as we position on track once more for a fresh year's work.

By October I am in the thick of paperwork again as invitations to foreign military performers must go off early if we are to be in line for consideration for next year's show. The American air force display selection commitee meets in December to consider all the air display invitations received from Europe. Only a small number are accepted. The USAF has to consider manpower, aircraft availability due to operational commitments and the logistics of getting to the display. If there is another major display nearby, you have a better chance of participation. Obviously priority is given to displays run at US air bases to support air force benevolent funds.

Air Spectacular has always been popular with American crews especially those of Irish descent and competition is hot between the squadrons to display in Ireland. The final confirmation of the aircraft types participating comes from the USAF just six weeks before the show.

Detailed planning of the type of programme we want to feature is well under way by late October and the booking of civilian acts begins. Choosing these acts is not as easy as it may seem. A number of factors have to be considered. Is the proposed display safe? Here we rely on feedback from our own observations of the individual's performance at other air displays. If the pilot is not known to us we check with other display organisers in England and Europe with whom we have close contact. The key factors are that the display is safe and offers good entertainment. Display pilots themselves are keen to weed out cowboy operations from the system because they taint the professionals and the entire scene. Slapdash performances endanger the safety of spectators and pilots alike. To help in this area the performers now have their own association which sets standards and keeps a watching brief on the industry as a whole.

When considering the proposed act's entertainment value we ask if it is something that the public will want to see. We must not just cater for the aircraft enthusiast but for the family out for a day's entertainment. Repeat acts and second rate performances are remembered.

The mixture of entertainments within the show programme is most important and it can take a lot of time at meetings to agree on the right balance. Aircraft with Irish connections are also sought, as are aircraft celebrating their anniversaries.

Casting the net each year to see what is new in the circuit I write to as many display promoters as possible. I also keep a close eye on the aviation press and specialist magazines, a lot of reading which I must confess is quite enjoyable. I also visit air displays whenever possible to see the talent on offer. People have remarked to me over the years what a terrific time I have travelling to these shows free of charge and being wined and dined as a special guest. One hates to shatter the illusion but sadly the facts are very different. The IAC is a totally voluntary body. It does not have the resources so if I wish to see other airshows I must travel at my own expense. There are many shows in the UK and if I am travelling there on holiday I normally take in a couple of air displays.

As well as noting the flying programme and talking to the pilots, you can see how other organisers are coping with the problems which are common to most displays. I usually return home from these visits with a full notebook and a renewed confidence that we are not doing too badly with our own Air Spectacular. Most large displays in England and elsewhere get considerable help from the armed forces with their huge resources of facilities and manpower. The local police forces also co-operate very closely with the organisers at the planning stages and are prepared to close off sections of motorways and roads, creating one way systems which are well policed and marked, in order to get traffic in and out with the least possible delay.

When we have made our final selection of display acts we try to get as many as possible individually sponsored, to defray the large cost involved. The larger vintage aircraft like Sally B, the B17, have operating costs of some £2,000 sterling per flying hour and as she is based in Duxford just north of London it can take well over an hour just to get to Dublin. Thankfully in this case the crew do not charge for their time. They do it for the enjoyment. All they ask in return is to be fed and given a place to lie down if it is an overnight. The Sally B crew consists of pilot, co-pilot, engineer and ground crew member. The bomb aimers and gunners went out with World War Two. Sally B has a much safer passage through the skies these days and serves as a flying memorial to those American pilots who gave their lives in those dark days of turmoil.

Costs for an aerobatic display act work out at about £800 sterling and other general entertainment acts come in at around £1,000, plus transportation and accommodation. At all times we have to try to get the best value for money and keep within the budget. The display-going public seems to be happy with our efforts but we always keep in mind that you are only as good as your last display. There is a lot of paperwork involved in my job of co-ordinating. The era of the computer has eased this somewhat. Word processing in particular can save a lot of time. Today's keyboards are a far cry from the stiff mechanical typewriter on which the first displays were processed. Now when I get bogged down in a particular piece of paperwork I can just switch programmes, load up the flight simulator disk and do a few circuits to clear the mind.

A considerable amount of time is spent on the telephone and this means my home phone as the Air Spectacular contact number and my home number have been one and the same through the years. The line tends to get very busy, particularly during the month before the show, with calls from early morning to late at night. No nine-to-five office hours here. At times the calls arrive at two and three o'clock in the morning from the west coast of America where callers failed to check their sun dials. Not funny when you are trying to get some sleep. At times one takes the infernal instrument off the hook in order to get a break. Then I bought an answering machine which accepts the calls when I'm out and allows one to process them in an orderly manner. My thirteen year old daughter is very businesslike in taking messages. When I arrived home one evening I found her in conversation with a F-16 pilot asking did he have a Top Gun award? When he asked to meet her on the day and presented her with his Squadron patch she was thrilled.

72 *In the Starter's Box at Fairyhouse. Left to right, Madeleine O'Rourke, Tom Hudson and extreme right Peter Hynes*

73 *Operations Caravan at Baldonnel*

74 A steady stream of cars

75 Crash Services on station

The recruitment of volunteers for display day is quite a task. The IAC secretary Ken Townsend had the unenviable job of gathering together the lists from each of the affiliated sporting groups of those who would help with the hundreds of tasks ranging from car parking to crowd control. The names on the volunteer lists constantly change right up to the day of the show. Even with these agreed changes a few people will let you down by not turning up at all or by leaving their post after a short time. We must all be grateful to the majority of the volunteers who realise the enormity of the task of getting Air Spectacular to work well in all areas and who remain in position until relieved. This dedication is what makes the show.

At every meeting our budgets are reviewed and all expenses closely monitored. A single bad financial decision can make the difference between a small profit or a loss. Sponsorship has eased this burden but as costs rise annually with inflation, the gate income barely allows us to keep our head above water. If a charge was made for our own personal time and effort the cost would be totally prohibitive. The ever spiralling costs of insurance cover for the show is a considerable burden on the overall budget. The premium to cover Air Spectacular is now one of the largest single outgoings and in the future this item will be a major problem for all shows and may decide whether or not an air display is possible in a particular location. Sad to think that insurance which was established to protect people has now become the tail that wags the dog.

As the show date moves closer planning meetings are held once or twice weekly and sub-committees are formed to deal with each of the specific areas.

As our learning curve increased over the years we managed to pre-empt many of the potential problems. But with a constantly changing environment new problems always arrived to test us and one could never button it down completely. In the airshow business you cannot afford to adopt the attitude that every contingency has been anticipated. We were always in the business to some degree of crisis management. Flexibility and a cool head are paramount.

We have always tried to produce a good quality Air Spectacular souvenir booklet, as informative and entertaining as we can make it for the public. Anton Mazer, a graphic designer by profession who was born in Holland, came on a visit to Ireland and liked it so much that he set up home and business here. Anton was involved in powered flying and luckily for us he volunteered his considerable design skills in 1982 to help produce a quality publication. His talents have been much admired as every year we have improved the quality of the booklet. The colour covers he designed for the '83 and '84 shows were particularly attractive. In 1987 we were able to include colour photographs on the inside pages to be used as mini posters. They were a great attraction for the youngers and were completely sold out. We have kept the advertising content down and include as much information as possible relating to the show and the IAC. I think we have struck the right balance over the years. The production of this booklet from start to camera ready artwork normally takes about three months. I book the advertisements, enough to cover the production costs as the booklet must be self financing before the printing presses roll. Anton and myself then work on script and photographs and he begins the layout. The printing is done during the week of the show with the list of ever changing acts going in last. Many times we have had to rip out material just before press as yet another aircraft goes unserviceable. The rule is to always have plenty of spare material on hand. Finally the souvenir booklets arrive on site and are placed in the hands of our eager scout sales team who will let you have one for £1 on the day.

Regulations governing a modern air display are much more stringent than in the heady barnstorming days of the 1930s. No flying of any kind is allowed above the spectators or the general enclosure at any time during the day. All display aircraft must operate a set distance from the crowd line and display along a line normally parallel to the runway which is designated the display axis. This is usually marked by cones and white arrows. Displays must have been rehearsed beforehand and all manoeuvres must be carried out at such a height and in such a manner as not to cause hazard. The high performance jets must not break the sound barrier. A plethora of windowless houses and well ventilated greenhouses in the area would be unthinkable. I prepare all this information in a formal twenty page document called the air display briefing notes which include maps of the display site, facilities available, general show information and so on. The briefing notes are sent to each participating pilot at least six weeks before the show. I also send out technical requirements questionnaires so that we will know what to supply on the day in the area of starter units, fuel, oxygen, accommodation and catering. A full safety briefing which show pilots on the field must attend is held one hour before the main display starts and display pilots enroute or flying past and not landing are briefed by telephone. Over the ten years of Air Spectacular I recall only one act which gave us cause for concern. On that occasion a particular pilot demonstrated recklessly, flying a vintage aircraft. He was never used again.

The organisers must provide adequate fire and rescue facilities on the field capable of dealing with anything from a hot air balloon to a 747 jumbo jet. At Fairyhouse we had tenders capable of producing foam, kindly provided by the Civil Defence and Aer Rianta. The Air Corps provided a rapid intervention vehicle. We had a fire officer at the ready throughout the show, dressed in fire proof suit with a fully equipped rescue helicopter standing by to take him quickly to any crippled aircraft that might crash-land beyond the racecourse. A disaster plan is prepared before every display.

We have regular meetings with the Department of Transport to keep them fully briefed, to discuss content and to co-ordinate airspace requirements for the show. This is important because for example an F-16 high performance jet can use up a lot of airspace during its manoeuvres and then shift upstairs to twenty or thirty thousand feet in a matter of seconds. Sunday is one of Dublin Airport's busiest days and so advance planning is essential to avoid conflicting traffic. We value the close co-operation we get from the Department in planning the programme. This co-operation is essential for such a complex display. We aim for a spectacular show but it must be safe.

After the press conference which is usually held one month before the show I always feel there is no turning back now. The country knows there will be a show. Whether it will be the one described so completely at the press conference nobody can be certain. If a week is a long time in politics — it is even longer in air show organisation. The days roll by, the running order changes and changes again. The computer is in its element and the printer produces the updates with alarming speed.

The press coverage brings a sudden surge of interest. We get queries from coach operators, planning tours from all over Ireland, regarding access for their buses to the show. Aviation enthusiasts from abroad are also very interested in attending our only major international air display. It is their only opportunity to see the Irish Air Corps in action. The Corps is restricted and does not travel or participate in international displays abroad.

Air Spectacular is highly regarded abroad for its mixture of all aspects of aviation, for its novelty items and its fast pace. The high degree of professionalism is also appreciated. The visiting enthusiasts charter aircraft or arrive by scheduled airline or by sea. By all accounts they have a great display day Irish style.

Publicity regarding the show's visiting air forces has also brought protests from CND, the Irish Campaign for Nuclear Disarmament, who object to the introduction of NATO fighter jets to Irish air displays. The issue is debated in the letter pages of the Irish newspapers over the following weeks. I respect CND's right to object and the IAC has offered them space in the general enclosure to distribute leaflets on their aims and objectives. The IAC is in the business of displaying aviation in all its forms to the public and in surveys carried out over the years two of the most popular items are the aircraft from the foreign air forces and our own Air Corps. Air Spectacular is a family day out and provides a unique entertainment. Other neutral countries including Switzerland, Austria and Sweden feature aircraft from many nations and air forces in their air displays. All the top jet aerobatic teams are operated by air forces. To exclude them would be to eliminate a large segment of airshow entertainment. The display spectator wants variety and spectacle. Our customers are discerning. They want the best and we do our utmost to provide it.

A time I particularly dread is when the show "free admission" passes have been printed. These admit our many workers and their families and those who have helped the show in some way. Show sponsors are also allocated an amount. Passes must be strictly controlled but the bees gather around the honey pot. I discover friends I never had, who ring me out of the blue. Others who are silent all year suddenly pick up the phone. It is the same story. "Any chance of a pass?". But the answer is also the same. "No." Some take it quite badly. There is of course no point in slaving away for a year preparing for this one very special day, our only opportunity to raise funds for sporting aviation and then needlessly succumb to a clutter of undeserving freebees. One feels they just get in everyone's way.

Out at the display site the preparation of the facilities has been progressing for some time. Water, toilets, communications, power and tents appear among the long lists. In Baldonnel all facilities have to be laid in. Before the IAC can move equipment on to the field the necessary ceremony of "marching in" must take place. This is an army term for the eminently sensible arrangement when the Dept. of Defence representative for lands, the station commander, the grass contractor who has the rights to the grass on the field and a representative from the IAC come together and walk over the two hundred acres one week before the show and agree on the condition of the land. After this agreement the land is officially handed over to the IAC. The "marching out" takes place the following week when the same team gets together to agree what level of damage has taken place to fixtures and surfaces and to check that all the litter has been removed. This is extremely important. A wayward soft drinks can whisked into the jet intake of a Fouga can devastate the compressor blades and indeed endanger the lives of pilot and crew.

Paddy and his team are kept busy ensuring that the show access areas are clear and that all facilities are in place and in good order. The enclosure is roped off and barriers put into position. Sorting out the concession applications, from baked potatoes to encyclopaedias, is also Paddy's responsibility. His wife Irene is kept busy at home, fielding last minute applications as Paddy deals with the problems on site. He works late into

76 Control Tower at Baldonnel

77 Plenty of Toilets

78 Aircraft Static Park

79 Road Construction Team take a break

Saturday night to make certain that all is ready. One particular evening around 10.30 just before a show at Fairyhouse, manager Norman Colfer was doing his final tour of inspection before heading for home. Suddenly the sound of hammering echoed across from one of the racecourse buildings. He went over to investigate. "I might have known that it was you," he said discovering Paddy hard at it, putting the finishing touches to the commentary and ATC position.

By Saturday evening the display site resembles a well appointed village. It must offer just as many facilities to its prospective one day population. The provision of medical and first aid cover is most important. On Saturday Dr. Colm Killeen runs through his final checklist of equipment. He and his wife Ita have provided medical cover at all the Air Spectaculars to date as well as at many other air displays around Ireland. Dr. Killeen produces a medical emergency plan for the day and has a fully equipped surgery on the field at Baldonnel. Five first aid tents are spread about the general enclosure to cater for the huge crowds. The tents are in radio communication with each other and staffed by the Order of Malta. There are ten doctors and surgeons on call on the field. At Fairyhouse there were no tents: we had a purpose-built medical centre right beside the parade ring. During the previous week Dr. Killeen has checked with the hospitals which will be on call during the day and made the necessary arrangements should we have to evacuate a casualty by helicopter.

At the 1987 Air Spectacular we almost had our first air show baby. The mother was selling her wares to the public on the day and business was brisk. Although she had a notion she was going into labour she kept on working and cut things really fine. She was rushed to the Coombe Hospital where the baby was born virtually on arrival.

Each display brings its own problems. The first year of the US military jets brought in a few raised blood pressure cases. However the more usual medical problems range from sprains and cuts to asthmatic attacks from the newly mown hay on the field. In 1986 and 1987, when we had hot weather, a gallon or so of calomine lotion was administered to sunburned bodies despite incessant warnings over the public address to cover up. It was gloriously hot. The Killeens remember a lady who came and asked for a complete examination "now that you are here." Another asked for the pill. The Order of Malta first aid team in between more urgent duties were quite busy making up baby's bottles and cups of reviving tea. Lost children gravitated towards the medical tents and one or two parents, assured over the public address that their little ones had been found, grabbed an hour's respite and nonchalantly collected them at the end of the show. This of course is a miserable practice as it ties up medical staff in baby minding roles. One child deliberately mislaid for the entire afternoon kept asking "am I found yet?" Ita Killeen lays in a supply of sweets for these eventualities. With the Killeens in charge of things medical we never had to worry. They are the calibre of dedicated people who make the impossible seem normal and generate enthusiasm among those who may be faltering under the load. The doctors never see the air show and wait until Monday to hear about it from their patients. In voluntary groups the hardest workers see little of the end product.

Over in ATC the facilities provided by Baldonnel control tower are a far cry from the five by seven foot wooden box at Fairyhouse. In hindsight it was amazing that Peter and Liam with so little equipment, could produce an international air show from that same wooden box. They enjoyed so much the challenge of this one day, such a contrast to their normal civilised environment at ATC Dublin Airport. Not so with Air Spectacular at Fairyhouse. Here the rule books were thrown out. Here they were drowned by rain and frozen by the cutting wind like the rest of us, packed like sardines in the small wooden square trying to calm some irate visiting pilot who had just been told he must wait his turn in the queue before departure from the field. The traffic they dealt with ranged from ponderous balloons to high speed formations of jets. Peter and Liam could only finally relax after the last aircraft had departed the field and disappeared into the sunset. Dublin Centre radar could relax a little at that point also with no more blips popping up on their screens in all directions as the show reached its peak and display aircraft were approaching from other airshows. Dublin Centre must direct all this activity together with their normal Sunday traffic. The objective of ATC is to expedite the safe movement of aircraft within its operating area and without all their patience and co-operation it would not have been possible to produce such a slick, safe and exciting show.

At the rehearsals on Saturday, display director Tom Hudson, who has been busy for weeks writing and rewriting the sequence and timing of the acts, can check on final timings to ensure that the show runs to the last second. Accurate timing is essential if Air Spectacular is to keep on schedule all the way along and dovetail with the various fixed slots in the programme. These slots cannot be disturbed as they concern aircraft enroute from other displays and scheduled to begin their display with us at a fixed time. They may not be able to hold, due to available fuel load. The military jets in particular gobble up tons of fuel at an enormous rate and cannot be delayed. After Air Spectacular they may be off to meet another fixed slot at their next display appointment on the same day. Four displays per day would be normal for these aircraft. The rest of the programme must be built around the fixed time slots.

Down on the ramp our show commentators Mike Kelly and Liam Byrne are busy catching up on the last minute details from the pilots and Liam is recording interviews for use on the public address while the pilot is displaying the next day. Commentary adds a very important dimension to the show. It must be informative but also entertaining. Striking the right balance is the mark of a good commentator. Mike and Liam have been the backbone of our commentary over the last number of years. Mike's varied background in aero sports gives him a wealth of experience to draw on. He started to fly gliders in 1968. He qualified as a military parachutist in 1970 and got his private pilot's licence in 1976. By 1982 his interest included hang gliders and microlights. He is currently doing a course on aerobatics. Because the show comes around only once a year he does not get the opportunity to practise commentating. The weeks leading up to Air Spectacular and particularly the few hours preceding the start are therefore most stressful and nerve wracking. Once the show gets underway things tend to settle down, including the nerves. Liam Byrne who is very much the man with the facts and figures at his finger-tips is there to share the burden of the long afternoon. Careful pre-planning by both of them is most important. They will be the voice of Air Spectacular on the day.

Finally it is the eve of the big day, the one we have been planning for all year. When I get back from the field the evening is spent nervously pondering the weather forecast, the one thing we cannot organise. In between I run through check lists and work out last minute details on the display programme. Many of the visiting pilots have been taken out to see the town, a pleasure unfortunately forgone by the show organisers who must be bright eyed and bushy tailed for the long day ahead. Having packed the equipment and files to be taken to the field next morning it is time to collapse into bed for a few hours sleep. This sleep is normally fitful and the dreams alternate between the show organisers' three night-mares, an accident, bad weather and no crowd. Awake early Sunday morning. My stomach is in such a knot and I am in such a rush that break-fast is given a miss apart from a quick cup of tea. After yet another weather update it is time to head for the airfield. I aim to be there at 07.30 hrs. This is a nice time to be on the field. Everything is quiet. All the assorted stalls and tents look colourful with flags fluttering in the early morning breeze. The field is truly a small village. Occasional bird-song breaks the stillness of the morning while the parked aircraft stand silent awaiting the arrival of their masters who give them life.

The early public arrivals are parking patiently in a line outside the air-field gates. Some have travelled a long distance. They are determined not to miss a second of this very special day by making sure of a prime viewing spot. A group of youngsters on bicycles are ready and waiting with binoculars to record the registrations of the aircraft as they arrive over-head. As the crowds start to gather the last of the volunteer workers arrive. The seasoned ones will have brought the all weather gear which includes suntan oil, wellies and sandwiches. They may not be relieved for some time to go the main food tent for their meal. Car parking teams who have already marked out the parking areas with ropes and stakes are getting their final briefing. Stall holders are putting the final touches to their stands, the smells of the first burgers to be fried waft on the wind as the fast food vans open for business. Suddenly the birdsong is silenced as the public address crackles into life and background music helps us in our work. Ten o'clock comes and the gates are opened to the incoming flood which will continue non stop until well into the afternoon. The cash collectors and stewards work hard to keep the flow moving as quickly as possible. There is no going back now. Ready or not Air Spectacular has begun. The fruits of our year of planning are being put to the test. We are on the playground slide and we will hurtle to the end.

The radio set which is attached to you for the day comes to life with a disembodied voice offering you the first of many problems to be sorted out. How did organisers survive before the invention of the mobile radio? Over in display control the phone starts ringing. One extension is assigned to answering questions from the public. How much to get in, when does it start, what planes are coming and can granny get in free? An endless flow of routine questions. By the end of the first hour the operator's throat is dry. The other line is busy with queries from display pilots en-route asking for details on weather and final act times. At Baldonnel, "display operations" is located at the base of the control tower in a four-teen foot caravan. This contains a full computer set up, photocopying facility, Eircell mobile telephone and a myriad of radios linked to ground and air communication nets. There is an emergency 220 volt generator on the ground outside to cater for a mains failure. The caravan also contains an endless supply of 7up and biscuits for starving pilots who ramble by.

On the crowd side the information desk is kept busy dealing with both public and static exhibitors' queries as well as tasking the volunteer man-power. The village is teeming with activity. Even the police are installed in their own area complete with a makeshift jail. There is plenty of activity to entertain the public with aircraft arriving from all over Ireland and Europe and the first of the pleasure flights are taking to the air. At Bal-donnel we are able to offer the choice of a flight in an Islander, a DC3 or a helicopter. The morning seems to pass in a flash and suddenly it is time for the show briefing which is normally held at 12.30 hrs. with all the display pilots on the field attending. The met forecaster gives us his expected weather and we get the final draft of the programme of acts. If

the wind is over ten knots the hot air balloons will not be able to fly. If
the wind is fresh the parachutists, microlights and gliders will be grounded.
If there is a significant crosswind on the main runway some aircraft may
not land and will have to display overhead and depart. Some vintage aircraft types may not perform at all. The wind is a great ally but can be a
powerful enemy as well. If the cloudbase is low all the high level aerobatics will be affected. Capt. Bill Howarth gives the safety briefing and
then we agree on the final times, content and sequence of events with
the assembled pilots. This ends with the inevitable "check your watches
please" and a time check is given. This is important. All our watches must
agree. The pilots depart for a quick snack lunch as Tom Hudson and I
draft what we hope will be the very final, final programme of flying events.
No lunch for us. There is a great temptation to take some time off during
this final hour before the start of the main display and stuff the babbling
radio with its ever more pressing demands for your instant attention into
the nearest waste paper bin.

13.59 hrs. We are in the sardine can counting out the last precious
seconds. 14.00 hrs. We're off and for the next three and a half hours all
hell breaks loose. Act after act dazzles the public gaze. None of them
notice the best act of all as the team in the sardine can performs at circus
pitch juggling with radios, stopwatches, telephones and loud hailers in
an heroic effort to orchestrate this aerial ballet. "First act gone overtime,
cut next act by two minutes, jet after that must display on arrival due to
shortage of fuel, need to clear the gliders for take off now if they are to
reach height before display slot, commentator needs more info on aerobatic act, what time are the F4s due from Isle of Man". The adrenelin
flows, the heartbeat increases, the excitement is intense. There is an
overflow of activity as everyone tries hard to cope with the ever changing
situation. Patience of a saint. Hands of an octopus. Nerves of steel. Give
me that microphone. Mike Kelly and his team are trying their best to
interface all this over the public address to the far side of the runway in
a cool calm and most professional manner.

It all gets sorted out because we have a disciplined approach to the job
in hand as do the performers, most of them anyway. The odd prima donna
occasionally turns up despite all the careful screening, is noted and will
not be used again.

The show ends and it is time to demolish that juicy melon so thoughtfully provided by Liam's wife Anne. After such a hectic day it is about
the only food we can digest. As the crowds depart the mopping up begins.
Pilots who are staying overnight are dispersed to their accommodation,
equipment is packed away, stories of the day are swopped as we go
about our tasks. Finally as twilight is ending and the field is gently wrapped

in the velvet cloak of darkness it is time to join the merry throng indoors for a welcome drink before going home for a luxurious bath, then bed. Air Spectacular is over for another year. I will be able to re-live the memories thanks to Paul Duffy, aviation photographer and editor of *Irish Aviator* magazine, who gives me hundreds of photographs taken at each year's Air Spectacular. But, for now, it is over.

80 Plane Spotting

6
The Showmen

Over the ten years of Air Spectacular, there have been many daring and courageous pilots who demonstrate amazing skills. These showmen give up their weekends over the Summer months to display and spend their Winters practising and perfecting new routines. The fees they charge to show organisers do not in any way reflect the massive commitment involved but do help to take the sting out of the high cost of insurance, maintenance and fuel. They fly at displays because they have a great love for it. They are not daredevils but masters of their art, worthy descendants of the barnstormers of the thirties who get their rewards from the roar of approval of the crowd.

Let us look at some of the better known showmen who have appeared at Air Spectacular over the years. Capt. Arthur Wignall was without doubt Ireland's favourite aerobatic display pilot not just at Air Spectacular but at the many other shows, field and gala days held all over the country from the late fifties onwards. Arthur was born in Stockport, Lancashire in February 1930. He started flying gliders at the age of eleven and was fully licenced by seventeen. He joined the RAF in 1949. The RAF was his aerobatic training ground and he was a member of an aerobatic team flying Prentices that displayed at Battle of Britain shows all over England in September 1951. In June 1953 he took part in the Coronation fly past over London for the new queen Elizabeth II. He was flying a Meteor Eight jet. In July 1956 he had the distinction of flying the last operational flight of the Spitfire in RAF service. In April 1957 he left the service having flown 1,621 hours in twenty different aircraft types.

Arthur came to Ireland in 1959 to work for an Irish charter company called Skycraft Air Services which specialised in banner towing and passenger charters. The manager was Joss Yates and his fellow company pilot was Bill Howarth. He set up home in Ireland and quickly became well known flying an Auster which towed advertising banners over sports events at Croke Park and Lansdowne Road. Joss Yates remembers Arthur as an extremely skilled pilot and conscientious employee. Arthur left

81 Arthur Wignall

Skycraft in October 1960 to join Aer Lingus where over the years he flew Viscounts, Friendships, Carvairs and 737s.

In 1966 he served for one year as secretary to the Irish Aviation Club. In 1967 he was one of the pilots involved in ferrying *The Blue Max* film aircraft to Ireland from France. He also displayed these planes at the Ballyfree air display in June 1967 for which he was show co-ordinator. In 1969 he took part in the London to Sydney air race with Tim Phillips, flying a twin Commanche. Between 1973 and 1977 he carried out contract work for Aer Lingus in the Middle East and in Africa. Retiring from

Aer Lingus, he flew for a short time with Executive Aircraft Services, an air taxi firm, before joining Avair, the commuter airline, on its opening day in 1979. He was a pilot on Avair's scheduled services flying the Shorts 330s and Beechcraft 99s. He again spent some time in Africa flying leased aircraft for Avair. It was here that he was involved in a hair raising incident when on approach to Luganda airport in Angola the aircraft in front of him was hit by a SAM missile and exploded in mid air. In September 1980 he achieved his life-long ambition to own and fly a Pitts Special. This is a very high performance bi-plane specially developed for aerobatics. Pitts S2A EI-BKA was air freighted from America and had its first flight over Irish skies in October 1980. The Pitts was to become an extension of Arthur. It was his pride and joy and this was reflected in the exuberance and skill of his displays with it. He spent many hours in the air perfecting the aerobatic routines and jogging daily to ensure the personal physical fitness which would enable him to endure the great stresses that aerobatic flying imposes on the human frame. During a typical aerobatic sequence of loops, rolls and spins, gravity forces of +6 to -4 can be experienced. +6G is the equivalent of having six people of your own weight dropping suddenly on to your lap, perhaps twenty times during a five minute display.

Arthur estimated that he lost about four pounds weight during each display. His brightly coloured Pitts performed its first display at Air Spectacular in 1981 and it was not long before a sponsor was found. EI-BKA became the Harp Pitts Special early in 1982. From then on the flying Harp appeared all over the country and aerobatics became very high profile with the Irish public. EI-BKA was the first high performance aerobatic aircraft to appear on the Irish aircraft register.

Arthur Wignall was founder member of the National Aerobatics Council of Ireland and was its first chairman. He always insisted that aerobatics was not showing off but was rather a demonstration of a pilot's skill. He was always keen to share his great love of flying and any pilot who cared to ask would be given the benefit of his vast experience. Interested groundlings also would be encouraged to have a go. On a personal note it was Arthur who introduced the author's daughter Marguerite to flying. He took her for her first flight in Kilkenny in June 1981. As a six year old she was very impressed. Sadly aviation in Ireland suffered a tragic loss on 1 April 1984. At a display held in Sligo in conjunction with a workshop session on aerobatics for student pilots, Arthur and his Pitts crashed. He was killed instantly. Air Spectacular and all the other air displays around Ireland will miss the sparkle that Arthur added in his own imitable way. It will never seem quite the same without him. He was Ireland's own display pilot.

The Vixen formation, Marcus Edwards and John McClean, flying open cockpit Pitts S2A Specials began a long and happy association with Irish crowds when they appeared at Air Spectacular 1982. They stunned the crowd with their breathtaking aerobatics which included the mirror formation in which one aircraft flies upside down in a mirror image only feet apart from the other. Their opposition flick rolls were superb. Marcus and John were both former Rothman's aerobatic team pilots who formed Vixen Two when the Rothman team disbanded in 1980. It is interesting to note that the Rothman's team was the first civilian aerobatic team in the world. Marcus and John bought their own Pitts aircraft from Rothman's and financed it entirely themselves. They started to make a living by flying full time. When not displaying they offered tuition in the art of aerobatics to flying schools and to individuals all over the British Isles. It was very hard work and the pilots' families were very much involved in making it successful. John's wife Judith, as well as being mum to their two children Rebecca and Dominic, was their most enthusiastic team manager. Whenever the opportunity arose the family would travel in the

82 John McClean (standing) and Marcus Edwards

two seater Pitts, sampling the thrills as well as the cold of the open cockpit. They became experts in the properties of thermal underwear and other
chill defeating clothing. Vixen Two was soon being recognised as among
the foremost aerobatic team in this part of the world. More enthusiastic
people one could not hope to meet. They delighted in doing a loop just
for fun. They enjoyed sharing the skills of aerobatics, even though they
both held commercial licences with thousands of flying hours between
them and could easily have opted for the secure life of airline pilots.

John McClean was born in Dublin in December 1941. He grew up in
Phibsboro, Dublin and attended the O'Connell School. His father had
served in the Merchant Navy. At the age of eleven John availed of a
Bristol naval scholarship at the Naval School in Ipswich. However, he did
not fancy a career with boats and applied at eighteen years of age to join
the Irish Air Corps. He was turned down because he had too many fillings
in his teeth. The following year he applied to the RAF and went to the
Cranwell Academy from which he graduated with honours. He started
his flying career with the RAF, piloting Vulcan bombers. In 1963 he
married London born Judith Newport and they started a nomadic life
over the following years as John was posted to different areas in the UK
serving in maritime command, flying Shackleton and Nimrod aircraft.
They finally set up home in Truro, Cornwall. After qualifying as a flying
instructor John was posted to the University of London air squadron.
On leaving the RAF in 1979 he was offered a position with Air UK but
opted to join the Rothman's aerobatic team which offered a much more
attractive opportunity – flying a Pitts Special.

Marcus Edwards was born in Brigend, Mid-Glamorgan, Wales. On leaving school he began his studies to become a vet before realising that his
true vocation lay in the skies. He joined the Royal Navy in 1962. He
served on the aircraft carrier HMS Eagle, flying Sea Vixen jet fighters.
He also flew with the RAF jet aerobatic team, the Red Pelicans, which
was the RAF's premier team until replaced by the Red Arrows. He then
became an instructor with the Jordanian Air Force. On returning to
England in 1977 he flew a Pitts with the Jubilee Duo. Marcus joined the
Rothman's aerobatic display team in 1978, leading the team in 1979 and
1980 when they toured all over England and the Middle East.

Vixen returned to Ireland in April 1983 flying for Rothman's at the
Circuit of Ireland Rally giving displays at Mondello Racetrack and at
Killarney spectator stages. For Air Spectacular 1983 Andy Wallbridge
from Blackpool, a reserve pilot on the Rothman's team, joined Vixen.
Now they had three Pitts Specials. Other displays followed in Ireland as
word of this fine act spread. Over Easter 1984, again in conjunction with the
Rothman's Circuit of Ireland Rally, Vixen pioneered an exciting new vari-

ation when they displayed over the river at Waterford city, co-ordinating their display with a formation of speedboats on the river. "Chicken Runs" and other exciting routines were performed. In June 1984 Rothman's brought John over to give a solo display at Sandycove, Co. Dublin, on the occasion of the Dun Laoghaire festival. John's display on Saturday 16 June was fifteen minutes of magic and he had the assembled crowd enthralled. It was to be his last display in Ireland. Just two weeks later on 29 June both John McClean and Andy Wallbridge were killed in a mid air collision over the sands of Morecambe Bay, Blackpool, where they had been practising for a display next day. The third member of the team could only circle helplessly in his Pitts as his friends crashed onto the beach. Marcus continued the spirit of Vixen by coming to Air Spectacular 1984 where he received warm applause as he gave a solo aerobatic display to open the show. A fine salute to the memory of his team mates.

Wing Commander Ken Wallis was born in Cambridge in 1916 and must surely be one of the most seasoned and vintage show performers around Britain since the early sixties. His interest in engineering and aviation was aroused early as his father and uncle had raced motorcycles of their own construction and had completed the world's first steel tube framed aeroplane in 1910. They called it the "Walbro" monoplane. In 1978 Wallis built and flew a replica of this machine, the original having been scrapped many years before. He got his pilot's licence in April 1937 and joined the RAF at the outbreak of war. He was an operational pilot flying Lysanders and among other tasks he had to fly many cloak and dagger missions behind enemy lines in France delivering and collecting members of the French resistance. He then graduated to Wellington bombers and was captain on thirty six missions over Germany and Italy. He had many close escapes including two crash landings, one when the Wellington had an undercarriage failure. On another occasion the bomber was damaged by flak but managed to limp back over England where the crew bailed out successfully. When the crew had jumped Wallis made his way from the cockpit to the exit at the back of the plane at which point he discovered that his parachute had snagged near the cockpit and had unravalled the length of the aircraft. As time ran out Wallis gathered the chute in a bundle, jumped out and threw the chute into the air. It opened correctly and carried him to a rough landing. On another occasion the Wellington flew into a barrage balloon cable. These cables were designed to bring down enemy bombers and now its serrated edges were sawing through the wing spars of the Wellington. The cable had cut through the first spar and was working on the second as the crippled bomber plunged downwards. Thankfully the cable broke before the spar had been severed. Wallis regained control and with the wing flapping gently he managed to put the aircraft down safely at the nearest airfield.

In between operation tours he instructed at operational training units and commanded a gunnery training flight. In 1945 he specialised in air armament and took a permanent commission in the newly formed technical branch of the RAF where one of his tasks was the evaluation of captured enemy aircraft. During this period he flew many aircraft types from single engined trainers to ten engined jets. The largest aircraft was the B36. He held a number of posts in the armament design establishment and many of his ideas and innovations have been adopted by the services. In 1964 Wallis retired from the RAF in order to continue the development and operation of his autogyro. In 1957 he had built a Benson B8M gyrocopter which he then modified using an improved control system. With the experience gained on this machine Wallis developed a completely new design which resulted in the Wallis WA116 prototype. This was a much refined, multi purpose autogyro, which could be safely flown hands and feet off and which incorporated a new device whereby the rotor could spin up by using the engine power before take off. The engine was a modified air cooled 72 hp. McCulloch, 4 cylinder, two stroke unit driving a two bladed propeller. It had a maximum speed of 22 mph. which allowed a full hover in light winds. This design started his crusade for wider usage and acceptance of the aerial motorbike, a cause he has been persistently devoted to for over thirty years. He holds all sixteen altitude, speed, distance and duration records for autogyros. In 1982 he set a new world record for altitude when he attained 18,504 ft. These records give testimony to the outstanding performance of the Wallis autogyro and the design is constantly being improved. Wallis' autogyro "Little Nellie" came to the public eye in 1966 when she was flown by her designer Wallis who was doubling as 007 in the film *You Only Live Twice*, a worthy successor to the already famous Aston Martin car used in previous films. As a double for Sean Connery, Wallis had to part with his beard and wear an open-neck sleeveless shirt. Flying at 6,000 ft. over mountains in early morning was a cold business. All the flying sequences were performed by Wallis who spent forty six hours in the air doing eighty five flights over the volcanoes of Japan and the rugged coastline of the East China Sea. Apart from the guns which fired only blank cartridges, the range of exotic weapons required for the 007 armoury were fired from the autogyro. These included guided missiles, rocket packs, flame throwers and parachute bombs. "Little Nellie" packed quite a punch and film audiences loved it. As a consequence of her popularity "Little Nellie" continued her star status and appeared in shows all over the world in her never ending battle against the nasty Spectre agents who ceaselessly invade airshows

83 Ronan Power tries "Little Nellie" for size with Wing Commander Wallis

to take pot shots at "Nellie" while she displays to her fans. By the end of 1987 "Little Nellie" had flown at 700 displays in the UK, the USA and Australia.

In a more serious role the Wallis autogyros have carried out many experimental flights with radar and infra red linescan equipment on board and have been used in ship based trials on British naval vessels with good effect. Wallis has shot nature film using the autogyro as a camera platform for TV and feature programmes. The machine is currently being assessed by the British Army for a possible military role.

Cdr. Wallis is a brilliant research and design engineer and holds many awards for his work. He is also a dedicated showman at Air Spectacular.

Richard Goode, aerobatic pilot extraordinary, is a man of great courage and determination. He rarely misses a display. He fought his way back to health and back into the air after a terrible aircraft accident. Many others would have thrown in the towel and taken up less arduous pursuits.

Thirty seven year old Goode is a successful management consultant who spends his weekdays dressed in pin stripe suit around the boardrooms of the world. At weekends in stark contrast, he dons blue flying suit and ascends into his true element. Aerobatics is his first love and he has become one of Britain's most spectacular display performers.

Richard Goode was infected by the bug in 1970 when a friend of his bought a Tiger Moth. He took instruction in it and aerobatics quickly followed. By 1976 he was experienced enough to give displays and in 1977 he purchased a Pitts Special and represented Britain in the 1978 World Championships for competitive aerobatics held in Czechoslovakia. Further competitive events followed, adding to his skill and experience. By the 1980 World Championships he was being placed well up the field with the best.

In 1981 Goode was appointed British team captain for the European Aerobatic Championships where he noticed that the new monoplane design, high performance, aerobatic aeroplanes were doing marginally better in competitions than the now long in the tooth Pitts Specials. He decided to purchase a monoplane as his next aerobatic machine. Goode had built and modified a derivative of the Stephens Akro aerobatic monoplane which he called the Pace Spirit. It was fitted with a three bladed propeller and a 270 hp. engine. The airframe was stressed to an ultimate load of + or - 16G.

It took to the skies in May 1982 carrying the appropriate registration G-OODO. During the airshow season all his spare time was spent practising his display routines, running four miles a day and abstaining from alcohol. Only in Winter was he free to indulge in the luxury of forbidden

84 Richard Goode

pleasures. Goode admits that he is not a natural born pilot and he has to work very hard at perfecting his skills especially after the long Winter rest. During the Winter the aircraft is exhaustively tested and completely overhauled. In competitive events he rates the flying ability required at 20%, the right aeroplane 10% and the remaining 70% as pure determination and commitment. To cover the high financial outlay Goode obtained sponsorship from Pace Petroleum. In 1983 he displayed for the first time in Ireland at Air Spectacular in Fairyhouse, emerging from the murk that surrounded the field after visiting friends at Powerscourt. His high performance Pace Spirit created great interest.

In January 1984 Pace Spirit was crated and travelled by sea to Australia to do a bit of upside down flying down under. Goode had been invited to take part in an international aerobatic event there. Twelve of the world's top aerobatic pilots came together for a feast of aerobatic flight which delighted the Australian public. By May 1984, back in England, Goode had all his sterling qualities put to the test when he crashed in Pace Spirit and sustained multiple injuries. He was making a flypast on Saturday 12 May at a friend's wedding in Saxmundham, when on a pull up manoeuvre he suddenly experienced severe vibration. On scanning the wings he saw that the leading edge of the left wing forward of the main spar was missing. Horrified witnesses on the ground could see bits falling from the aircraft. Goode managed to retain control of the aircraft for a brief period in a deep descending turn to the left but as the aircraft approached the ground and he attempted to raise the nose the rate of roll increased. Pace Spirit struck the ground on its left wingtip at an angle of 90 degrees. It continued along the ground for twenty five metres as the rest of the left wing disintegrated. It ended up inverted. There was no fire and Goode was released from the wreckage by onlookers and rushed to hospital. He suffered a dislocated hip and fractures to both legs. Pace Spirit was a total write off. He made a quick recovery and was officiating as a judge for the British nationals held at Cranfield in September. By early 1985 he had completely recovered from his injuries, had regained his pilot's medical certificate and was busy getting back into flying practice. His next appearance in Ireland was to be at Air Spectacular '85 in Cork but unfortunately, due to weather, he was not able to display. The weather relented in 1986 and 1987 and Air Spectacular was able to welcome this courageous pilot to Baldonnel where he flew his "Ultimate Pitts" G-OODI. Equipped with a 270 hp. engine it has the highest power to weight ratio of any aerobatic aircraft in Europe. It is capable of staggering performance and manoeuverability as the crowds were to appreciate.

He loves coming to Ireland where he says he is always assured of a warm welcome. This helps to dispel the memories of the long sixty mile sea crossing from England flying in a temperamental thoroughbred aerobatic aircraft. Unlike crossing the English Channel which is always packed with shipping, the Irish Sea always seems a lonely, cold and deserted place.

For the 1988 air display season, thanks to contacts in East Germany, he purchased a brand new aerobatic aircraft, the Russian YAK 50. The YAK 50s are used to great effect by the Russian aerobatic team and are seldom seen in the West. Exciting times for this very adventurous pilot.

Brian Lecomber was booked to attend the first Air Spectacular in 1978. He combines two of the most unlikely occupations of author and display pilot. As a writer of best selling thrillers and as a full-time professional pilot, he has a life almost as exciting as the heroes portrayed in his many books.

Brian was born on 12 July 1945 in London. He left school at the age of sixteen without any qualifications and joined the school of life. He became an apprentice mechanic with a company that raced BMW motor-bikes. Within a year boredom had set in and Brian decided to try the great outdoors, working in forestry. Encouraged by a school pal he decided to give journalism a try and joined a Buckinghamshire freelance news agency.

With the standard cub reporter's training he launched out into the unsuspecting Buckinghamshire community, pad and pencil at the ready searching for that elusive scoop. He specialised in reporting motoring events and became an aviation correspondent. While snooping around the local airfields looking for yarns he decided to have a go himself. He learned to fly a Tiger Moth at the Denham flying club. While still a student pilot he took part in a small flying circus and pioneered a no-parachute jump from the wing of a Tiger, using foam padding on impact. The first time he tried this stunt he banged in nicely, none the worse for wear. The second time he was not so lucky and ended up with broken bones. Having gained his licence and built up his hours aero towing gliders, he became an instructor at the Denham club.

Moving to Antigua in 1971 to join the local flying club as its chief instructor meant quite an adjustment for Lecomber. The club had one Cessna 150 and a box beside the runway containing a cracked spanner and a worn-out tyre. The club's financial situation was no better. Accounts were in the red. Brian settled in to make a go of it and clocked up 1,300 flying hours in the first year. He also visited some of the neighbouring islands to encourage pupils. Before the end of the year the bank accounts were in the black and two aircraft had been added to the fleet. While in Antigua, Lecomber finished a novel he had started in England. It was titled *Turn Killer* and told of a young pilot with a Denham based flying circus, who gets mixed up with the Mafia and goes to the Caribbean with murderous consequences. Lecomber himself had fallen foul of a mafia-type manager of a local casino and he became unpopular for a while. It looked for a time as though the healthy thing for him to do would be to go back to England. Luckily the manager moved to another island and died in suspicious circumstances.

When he returned to England in 1973 Lecomber submitted his manuscript to a publisher and resumed flight instruction and towing gliders. The book was accepted and Brian started writing full time. A second novel *Dead Weight* followed, again using the mix of personal experiences and fantasy. The proceeds from the books enabled Brian to purchase a Stampe and he started to practise aerobatics in earnest.

In 1977 he entered many of the major aerobatic competitions in England and carried off four trophies. By the end of the year he was writing his third novel *Talk Down* a thriller about a non-pilot faced with the task of landing a light aircraft after the pilot had become incapacitated. It became a best seller around the world and was serialised in the *Sunday Express*. In August 1978 Brian gave his first display in Ireland flying his brightly coloured orange and blue Stampe. His crazy flying routine was well received. Later that year he was invited to join the Rothman's aerobatic team, a call he could not refuse. He toured for two years with team leader Marcus Edwards, flying the Pitts S-2A Special. In 1980 he performed at 130 displays from Farnborough, England to the Middle East. When the Rothman's team disbanded Brian found sponsorship for his own Pitts Special G-BOOK and flew for four years in Dunlop colours. At the end of 1984 Dunlop pulled out due to financial problems, so in 1985 Toyota and Jaguar cars became his new sponsors.

A typical year starts in February after the Winter hibernation. This is the time for Brian to get back to grips with his Pitts display mount. He works himself hard to return to tip top display fitness. The Pitts with the 200 hp. engine is stressed to +9 and -6G. The pilot is held in the cockpit by a harness of six straps and has to wear a folded towel under the lap straps to prevent bruising during the negative G manoeuvres. When not in the air there is lots of paperwork. Technical documents relating to the aircraft, insurance documentation, personal licences, permits and clearances for the many upcoming displays. There are not enough air shows around the country so he flies also at fetes, carnivals, regattas, tattoos and other outdoor events of an aerobatic nature. Having convinced the organisers that their event would not be the same without his spectacular aerobatic display the real work begins. All the loose ends have to be tied up, maps of the area acquired, Department exemption obtained from the Civil Aviation Authority for the day, the police and the local authority informed, press releases, posters, handbills and commentary scripts sent on to the

85 Brian Lecomber and his Stampe

organisers. The personal planning for the day must also be worked out and with very special attention to time and distance it is possible to fit in up to four different venues in an afternoon. As Summer is the peak earning time, he cannot afford to turn anything down. Careful calculations must be made for fuel, smoke oil, time, daylight and other considerations.

By May teething problems with pilot and aeroplane have been sorted out and the display routines for the year fully rehearsed. Display variatons include both bad weather and good weather displays as well as a couple to suit the shapes of different display sites. Soon the display season starts in earnest. By late July half of the season has passed with over 100 displays performed, depending on weather. Each performance is more polished as plane and pilot become as one in the air. By the end of September both pilot and machine are feeling a bit worn, with a total of over 200 displays behind them. Thankfully the season has come to an end.

Brian sees himself as an entertainer in the skies and in print. His novels incorporate such realism in the flying sequences because he really does know how it feels up there and can convey this. He intends to keep up aerobatics with always the cushion of a career in writing. Brian sums it up quite philosophically, "If I have to give up flying I would like it to be in a ball of fire on a green English airfield at the age of 103."

Top place for the most unusual item at Air Spectacular '87 must surely go to Brendan O'Brien for his heart stopping truck top landing display in which he lands and parks a Piper Cub on top of a fast moving truck and trailer. This novel act was pioneered in America and first performed in Ireland by Brendan. Brendan lives by the code that variety adds spice to life. He is the only display pilot booked by Air Spectacular over the years who has turned up with three different acts. In 1984 he was flying with the Fournier Duo who demonstrated precision formation flying using powered gliders. In 1986 he was booked to fly a "girl on the wing" routine using his Tiger Moth but unfortunately a last minute snag with his aircraft prevented his appearance. In 1987 he performed the truck top landing.

Brendan's family came from Co. Carlow but his parents moved to London before he was born. Brendan was orphaned at the age of fourteen. His first contact with aviation was flying gliders as a youngster and he got his private pilot's licence in 1972. Air shows first became a part of Brendan's way of life in 1974 when he joined the Rothman's aerobatic team as commentator and ferry pilot. Having gained experience flying Pitts Specials he went on to display the type as a member of the Marlboro team. He then operated as a freelance pilot using his own Pitts Special. He made his first appearance display flying in Ireland with the Ford Pitts

86 Brendan O'Brien

Special at the world ploughing championships held in Kilkenny. His spirited display on that occasion had the farmers diving for cover. By 1982 Brendan decided that the rather frantic Pitts Specials were suffering from over exposure. He decided, with his background in gliding, to return to displaying the simple basic manoeuvres of his long wing Fournier RF4 aerobatic motor glider, stylish and elegant. The following year he joined forces with John Taylor to create the unique and much admired aerial ballet of the Fournier aerobatic duo, later to become the Unipart Duo, flying to the music of Pink Floyd. This act became very popular with display organisers, providing a lovely contrast of silent flight with lazy smoke trails compared to the thunderous roars of the other aircraft.

Brendan was very much the all round aviator having also qualified as a military parachutist. He took up the sport of hot air ballooning twenty years ago in order to relax and still continues this interest. During the Winter months he does aircraft ferry work taking different types of aircraft across the Atlantic and to far flung places. He has acted as expedition pilot on polar expeditions. A recent assignment has been with the British

Antarctic Survey, flying their research personnel and equipment out of Rothera Base in Antarctica.

When not in the air Brendan enjoys a diversity of interests; ornithology, entemology, photography, mountaineering and collecting books. He is entered in the *Guinness Book of Records* as holder of more world records than any other pilot. He recently established no less than 201 FAI speed records. While in America Brendan saw the truck top act and decided to bring it to Europe. He persuaded IVECO to give him their latest IVECO Ford seventeen litre, 420 hp. V8 Turbostar truck and to sponsor the act. Then he acquired a 150 hp. Piper Super Cub aircraft which could land on the forty foot moving runway. The roof of the trailer was specially reinforced. He had just three weeks to rehearse and perfect the stunt before it was airshow time. Its debut was at the Biggin Hill international air fair in Kent in June 1987. The press in an inspired piece referred to it as the plane that fell on to the back of a lorry. Brendan repeated it the following weekend before a French audience at Vichy. He has now successfully done it over fifty times. He is working on a new act for the 1989 season. For Brendan the challenge is working up and perfecting the display, performing it for a year or two then trying something new. It is this challenge that keeps him on permanent lookout for new ideas with which to thrill the air display spectators.

87 Air Corps Silver Swallows. Left to right, Capt. Jack Killoch, Capt. Kevin Barry, Lt. John Mulvany, Lt. Pearse McCrann

7
Baldonnel

Ever since we realised back in 1982 that the show had outgrown Fairy-house we decided to seek permission from the Minister for Defence to use Casement aerodrome as the most suitable home for Ireland's International Air Display. We had prepared a submission in the Summer of 1984 but when the request came from Aer Rianta to run the show in Cork we did not proceed. I had attended a display at RAF St. Athan just outside Cardiff, in September 1984. This show was of a similar size and had a layout and crowd numbers similar to what we could expect at Baldonnel. While there I carried out a feasibility study and came back with some useful information for the board. I was in no doubt now that a display run at Baldonnel would work. The advantages were many. Access was good from a dual carriageway, it was very near Dublin city and suburbs, the airfield was well equipped and had long runways capable of taking most of our display traffic. There was also a good static display area for public view. The grass area was huge, capable of swallowing up any crowd we could provide. People could see the action while remaining seated in their cars if they wished.

The drawbacks were obvious to anyone having to transform a bare field into a facility for 80,000 people. Toilets, catering, medical, tele-phones, barriers and tents would all have to be provided. This was a complete reversal of our situation at Fairyhouse. In addition some work would have to be done to improve access for cars entering the airfield and we would need the weather on our side to avoid cars getting bogged down in soft ground. The general officer commanding the Air Corps and Director of Military Aviation, General Brian McMahon, was well disposed towards the Irish Aviation Council and supported its aims and objectives. He had served on the board of the council in the early seventies. He was the recipient of the Distinguished Service Medal when rescuing an injured man by helicopter from a cliff face at Glendalough in March 1970 and was pilot on the delivery flight of the first Air Corps Alouette III heli-copters in 1963.

Even though Air Spectacular '85 at Cork had to be cancelled the Department was impressed by the organisation and planning of the event outside of Fairyhouse. It demonstrated that the IAC was capable of managing an event on a much larger scale than before and the Minister was now satisfied that we could meet the stringent requirements for security and crowd control. In January 1986 the council received the Minister's formal permission authorising the use of Baldonnel for Air Spectacular '86.

Lt. Col. John O'Brien, the Department's representative on the IAC since June 1982, guided us through the following months of planning and preparation. The construction of new entrances and exits and the improvement of roads surrounding the airfield was capably taken on by Paddy Byrne, Tony Murphy and the members and friends of SAAC. From homebuilders of aircraft they became road engineers for airshows. Airmotive kindly gave us permission to use one of its entrances as an access point. Litter would be a huge problem in such a large area. Capt. Kevin Byrne, a pilot with Aer Lingus and involved with the Air Scout movement, agreed to organise a party of scouts to take care of this. Our president, Tom Farrington, would look after hospitality over the weekend and secretary of the IAC, Ken Townsend, was in charge of administration. It took many months of hard work and endless meetings to sew it all up.

The co-ordination of the display acts was now quite a handful. The fact that a lot of aircraft would be landing at Baldonnel meant planning for the technical requirements as well. Such items as starter units, oxygen and fuel were high on the agenda. Accommodation was a big item as all the participating military teams had to be booked into local hotels and transportation laid on. Invitations had been sent to many national air forces including the USSR and the booking of the civil attractions was under way. The theme for 1986 was aviation from World War One to the present day. There was much debate in the press in early Spring as to whether or not the American F-111 swing wing bombers would be coming. They had been in action over Libya earlier in the year. By June we could confirm that the controversial jets would not be attending any European events in 1986.

Once again the legendary Irish Summer weather was causing concern. August '86 opened as one of the wettest ever. Just two weeks before the show, which was set for Sunday 17 August, there had been so much rain that the area intended for parking was waterlogged. At one of our meetings Liam Byrne remarked that at least the seaplane would be able to perform on the day. We could not contemplate a cancellation for the second year running although inevitably the suggestion was made. Cork had drained away all our funds although thankfully our weather insurance had covered the major portion of our losses.

The sun shone on Sunday 17 August. It turned out to be the best day of the 1986 Summer. The gates were open from ten o'clock and a steady flow of cars proceeded to the field. This was to be the first public air display to be held at Baldonnel since 1961. With the rush around lunchtime the entrances came under severe pressure. The crowds were the biggest ever recorded at Air Spectacular. We had to cater for over 70,000 people so entry to the field was a little slower than we would have wished. Some people impatient at having to queue, once inside just parked their cars anywhere and disappeared with picnic baskets before our harassed stewards could direct them to the proper parking area. Their action made our task of keeping a good traffic flow even more difficult. Indeed some people parked illegally on the Naas dual carriageway at vantage points overlooking Baldonnel and this also added to the traffic conjestion.

Teething problems we certainly had. But this happens with any new venue before the system has been tested. Baptism by fire? Yes, it certainly was. Even the toilet facilities became a cause for complaint. Some people thought the hessian tent toilets were the only facility available for both male and female use. Unfortunately many of the ladies had not seen the large block near the entrance which had been reserved for them. Because of the restricted availability of running water on that side of the field, we had to locate the ladies block near a rising main. Solving this problem would be top of the list for 1987.

We had to open yet another gate for people who wished to leave early with cantankerous children or to discover whether the oven was on or off and who were forcing their way out against the incoming tide. However most of our spectators survived all this and settled down to enjoy the show in lovely sunshine. Poor Mike was hoarse on the public address as children seemed to develop wanderlust and before long both the lost children centre and the medical tents were awash with offspring. One two-year-old took off all his clothes in the prevailing heat. The distraught mother found the clothes but not the child and thought the worst. Mike made an announcement ordering everyone to stop what they were doing and look around for a stark naked child. It worked. Paddy Byrne, Ken Townsend, Neil O'Byrne, David Tyndall and Kevin Byrne who made up the team in the general enclosure were up to their eyes. Before lunch Terry Rowan took to the air courtesy of Irish Helicopters to see just where the traffic log jams were. The situation began to ease. At the back of the field the members of MACI ran a display of control line and radio control model flying. Hot air balloons had their roped off section nearby and the public had a close-up view of the art of balloon inflation and thethered flight.

As for the flying display each had his or her own highlight and there

was a great variety to choose from. The long Winter months of research-
ing the line-up had borne fruit. The result was a true vision of aviation
from the early years to the latest high tech F-16. It was a once only chance
for most spectators to see a demonstration of aviation through the years.
The World War One Fokker Triplane a la Red Baron had first attracted
my attention at a display in England the previous year. I asked the pilot
how he would fancy a trip across the Irish Sea to display at Air Spectacular
to an enthusiastic crowd. "I'd enjoy that," he said and I made a provisional booking on the spot. Robin Bowes took over two days to complete the trip as his triplane wings battled against the headwinds. The
risky part of his journey was the sea crossing: there was no room in the
single seater for a survival dingy. This is what real performers are made
of. He looked quite exhausted when I took him to his accommodation
that night. Why did he do it? It was the usual reply. "To entertain the
crowds and show them what this unique aeroplane sometimes called the
flying venetian blind is capable of."

Another arrival on the Saturday was the two seater Spitfire, making a
nostalgic return to Baldonnel. It was ex-Air Corps No. 162 which had
been operated by the Corps from 1951 to 1968 when it was sold for use
in the Battle of Britain film. Nick Grace bought the aeroplane in 1979
and restored it beautifully to flying condition. This Spitfire had of course
flown in the real Battle of Britain and did a total of 174 sorties with the
RAF during the war. The Air Corps officers who had flown in No. 162
turned out to see the return of a Spitfire to her old home at Baldonnel.
By Sunday morning there was an impressive static display of aircraft for
the public to view. The field looked good in the most welcome sunshine.
As I was escorting one pilot to the briefing he asked how much it had all
cost. About £60,000 I said. He was aghast. "You're joking," he said. "In
England to set up a show of this size would cost twice that amount." I
explained that all the organising committee from the IAC and over 500
volunteers from our affiliated groups gave their services free of charge.
He stopped dead and looked at me but I rushed on to the briefing room
not waiting for the lecture on sanity which was about to come.

Over on the air display control sector things were hotting up. With the
display briefing over we moved to the control tower to start the main
show at 13.30 hrs. Air Atlantique was busy giving pleasure flights in the
unique DC3. ATC Baldonnel was fully occupied with over seventy private
aircraft on the field as well as display acts that had been arriving during
the morning. Iona National Airways towed banners welcoming all to Air
Spectacular '86. Not to be outdone Darby Kennedy of Weston showed
the crowd some real airmanship flying his school's Rallye. British Airways presented their 737 G-BKYL piloted by Capt. Ian McGrath. The

88 *"Nostalgic Return". Ex-Air Corps 162 Spitfire with owner Nick Grace*

89 *Captain Darby Kennedy*

aircraft was flying empty from Dublin in between passenger flights. After his display we dubbed it the aerobatic 737. Richard Goode who by now felt that he had used up seven of his lives showed us that he had not lost the touch in his Pitts. The F-16 display flown by USAF pilot Major Beltz had his G-suit working overtime. He had already completed two shows that day leaving Dublin Airport to display at Alconbury in England and then on to Nottingham before coming to Baldonnel. He began his fine display with a high speed pass at 550 knots before pulling vertical and into a half Cuban Eight. The F-16 can pull up to +9G and the pilot reclines in an almost at rest position of thirty degrees to help him withstand the high stresses produced by these manoeuvres. The F-16 is controlled by the latest fly-by-wire technology and uses a single stubby control stick between the thumb and two fingers of the pilot's right hand requiring just a touch to get a response.

A G-suit is most essential for high speed jet aerobatics. The anti-G inflates a balloon type bladder around the pilot's waist and legs and by pushing against that with his muscles he can actually force the blood back into his head and prevent black out. Fly-by-wire is a new system of sending information to the hydraulic and electro-mechanical muscles which control the aircraft's moving parts. The tiny control stick translates the pilot's finger movements into electronic pulses, greedily gobbled up by the control microprocessor which in turn issues orders to the associated systems at the speed of light. Confirmation of the action appears immediately in the head up display so the pilot does not have to look at the instruments and can concentrate completely on the view out the window.

What a contrast to the F-16 it was when the wooden wonder of World War Two, the Mosquito, appeared flown by Tony Craig, the only surviving example in the world and owned and operated by British Aerospace. The two Merlin engines were like sweet music to the ear. The Spitfire was then displayed by Nick Grace before the Irish Air Corps took to the air to present their first Air Spectacular display on home ground. Their twenty minute display introduced the first three of the newly delivered Dauphin helicopters. Aer Turas CL44 flown by Capt. Nigel Budd landed, made a three point turn at the far end of the runway and took to the air once again. It was a day of nostalgia for the Air Corps as the next item was another aircraft type which had seen long service with them. The Vampire G-VTII was making its second appearance at Air Spectacular. The previous occasion had been at Fairyhouse in 1980. At Baldonnel she was displayed by Stan Hodgkins before departing back to her base at Cranfield in England.

The growl of the twin Hercules engines of the French Air Force Noratlas announced the departure from the field of the French Air Force

90 *French Airforce Noratlas*

91 *Irish Government HS125 Jet*

92 *Member of French Team*

parachute team. After climbing for altitude sixteen members of the team jumped together in free fall and performed a variety of geometric figures while descending at a vertical speed of between 180 and 280 km. per hour. Coloured smoke highlighted their tracks before they detached and deployed their parachutes to land in front of a cheering crowd. Their jump platform, the Noratlas has been in service with the French Air Force for thirty four years. The pilot Commandant Charles gave a short display which finished with a dramatic steep descent from 1,000 ft. to the runway and a perfect landing. Observing this from the tower we thought that he had left the "pull up" a little too late and would bounce down the runway with the undercarriage working overtime. We were wrong. Here was a master at work. For 1986 the commentary team was located with us on the balcony of the control tower and a distance from the spectators on the far side of the runway. Mike and Liam had to call the control point on the far side from time to time to determine if the audience was cheering, clapping or whatever. From the tower they could not see the crowd reaction. Mike found this isolation a little unsettling. He felt more comfortable when able to judge the crowd's reaction to the different acts.

The French Air Force Alpha jet flown by Lt. Philip Cartignies, on his first visit to Ireland, gave a polished performance, no doubt fortified by the draught Guinness he had sampled on Saturday night and found to his taste. Aer Lingus brought along the beautifully restored Dragon flown by Capt. J.J. O'Sullivan. The Italian Air Force's solo MB 339 jet brought gasps of amazement and admiration from pilots and public alike as Major Andrea Canetto performed the jet tailslide. This is a spectacular and very hazardous act. Climb at full power then point the nose at the sky and let the airspeed drop to zero. The aircraft comes down tailpipe first. Unless in expert hands the jet engine might suffer a flame out and with no engine weight in the nose to pull it over it could continue falling out of control until it hit the ground. The Red Baron in his Fokker was a stark contrast as he looped his World War One Triplane. The Widgeon, a small yellow seaplane, put its wellies away for the day and used its undercarriage to land on the runway. It was flown by its owner Michael Durkerly and was the only one of its type in Europe. With over forty different aircraft displays featured during the afternoon the show ended on a suitably quiet note with the two powered gliders led by John Taylor performing their aerial ballet set to music which wafted through the public address loudspeakers.

It had been a memorable day for all who had joined in Ireland's biggest family picnic in glorious sunshine at Baldonnel. The lucky ones who had pleasure flights in the helicopters or the majestic DC3 had tales to tell. One's hope is that among all those contented people a few would be filled with the love of aviation, a sport that puts you in a new and wondrous environment, riding on the winds and playing hide and seek among the clouds. At the end of the day that is what Air Spectacular is really all about. It is a shop window on what is possible, what can be done. For one day we lift the curtain to give a glimpse of what may become a lifetime of enjoyment. Flying is for everyone. We hoped we had inspired some to get out there and enjoy it.

The final American contingent left Dublin with the F-16s on Monday. Normally the controllers over the years at Dublin Tower are treated to a miniature air display as the departing military jets do a few beat ups of the airfield before setting course for home. No beat up could be facilitated for the departing F-16s in 1986 due to heavy line traffic, nevertheless the two jets managed a spectacular departure blasting down the main runway at Dublin Airport in formation, afterburners spitting fire and reaching a height of 4,000 ft. by the airfield boundary. The controller lazily urged the next departing flight, a British Airways BAC One Eleven, "Follow that if you can."

With renewed enthusiasm we set to the task of correcting the two major problems of '86, the traffic and the toilets. To solve the traffic conjestion we opened more entrances. Tony Murphy and SAAC built a new road across two fields, with the kind permission of the landowner Mrs. Alexander, and opened up a new access to the aerodrome. We would try to get the message out once again advising people to come early and make a day of it and above all to avoid the last minute rush. Sorting out the toilet situation involved a considerable outlay of money as we had to construct semi-permanent toilets on site with water laid on. When I assured the *Irish Times* columnist Kevin Myers that all would be well on the public convenience side of things, it prompted him to wonder in his *Diary* how the public managed during Daniel O'Connell's monster meetings more than a century ago. Maybe people took a more robust attitude to bodily requirements and attended to them as the need arose. Alas long gone, he proclaimed.

In an attempt to distribute the tremendous workload more fairly among the committee it was decided to break the areas of responsibility into clearly designated managerial sections. Tom Farrington was chairman. Lt. Col. John O'Brien was Air Corps liaison and vice-chairman. Tom Hudson and myself would handle air display operations. Ken Townsend took on general administration and was assisted by Paul Chamberlaine. Paddy Byrne would be in charge of services and Peter Hynes and Liam McCobb were the IAC Air Traffic co-ordinators. Kevin Byrne and Cliff Lebioda took charge of the static park. Terry Rowan had IAC publicity, Peter Schweppe, Denis O'Hogan and Brian Kearney, gate control. Bill

Howarth would be technical advisor and look after show briefing. David Tyndall and Larry Flood would be responsible for the car parking areas and Dr. Colm Killeen would again head up medical services. Oliver McCann was Aer Rianta's representative on the board.

1987 was a special year for our sponsor Aer Rianta. It was celebrating its fiftieth anniversary and it would be a most fitting present for Chief Executive Martin Dully and his team to be part of Ireland's largest and most spectacular air display ever. Air Spectacular would have reason to celebrate too because with crowds of over 125,000 it was about to become Ireland's biggest one day outdoor event.

The show organised by the Irish Aviation Council for Sunday 16 August 1987, the tenth Air Spectacular, was comparable to any of the other major displays held around the world. The star act which everyone came to see was the first ever appearance of the Red Arrows, the Royal Air Force's premier aerobatic team, who were flying their gleaming red Hawk jets. This was the first display by the RAF in the Republic of Ireland since the foundation of the State when the RAF 100 Squadron, flying Bristol fighters, withdrew from Baldonnel in 1922. There was controversy in the press about the Red Arrows' forthcoming appearance. People did not realise that they would have taken part in Air Spectacular in 1985 had the display been in Dublin. When we moved to Cork the extra distance made it impossible because of their other commitments on that day. We had to wait two more years before the world's top aerobatic military precision team could visit us at Baldonnel. It was their 88th show of the 1987 season and it was well worth the wait.

Once again Air Spectacular was blessed with good weather. It was Dublin's hottest day of the Summer with temperatures in the eighties and the crowds came out in their thousands. Traffic was heavy with tailbacks for many miles, but at least it was moving in a constant flow towards the airfield entrances. Some locals realised that this air show attraction could earn money so they opened up fields around the aerodrome, put signs up to guide the traffic and made a handsome profit at our expense. One lady innocently parked in an unofficial site and was directed to the show through a barbed wire fence. Having negotiated this obstacle she arrived at the information tent and, still convinced it was an official car park, asked if there was an easier way out to her car.

While the main show was not due to start until 13.00 hrs. there were several fly pasts by various aircraft. The show schedule had become so packed that this was the only time available to fit them in. There were many there to see these early attractions and to enjoy the entertainments in the general enclosure. The public had finally got the message and were coming early. One interesting static aircraft on display was the German

Air Force Transall which was visiting Ireland to collect two engines from a Focke-Wolfe Condor which had crashed in 1942 close to Mount Brandon in Co. Kerry while on a maritime patrol. All six crew members survived and its pilot Ernst Mollehauer, who spent the rest of the war interned with his crew at the Curragh Camp, had come with the Transall to accept the return of part of his aircraft. The engines were due to be put on display at a defence museum in Hamburg.

At 12.20 hrs. an Aer Lingus Jumbo EI-ASI with an RTE camera crew on board did some high and low speed passes. Aer Turas, a long time supporter of the display, did two passes with its DC8 which was on a positioning flight to Stansted to operate a bloodstock charter to Australia the following day. Four USAF F-16s enroute to their base in Germany from Spain dropped down to do a formation flypast at Baldonnel before continuing their journey. Club Air, flying the Boeing 727, did a fast flypast as did Ryanair with chief pilot Mike O'Brien at the controls of their BAC One Eleven. Peter Hynes, our ATC controller, showed that he was also a dab hand at aerobatics when he gave a nice display flying the Decathlon. Sally B, a B17 with pilot Keith Sissons on board moved from the static park where she had created much interest, being one of the last few airworthy B17s in the world. After a solo five minute display she was joined by the USAF A10 flown by Capt. Sean Jessurn for a unique formation of 1940s and 1980s flying machine technology. Capt. Jessurun did some skilful flying to keep a tight formation with the B17 before giving a solo display. This pilot's entire Summer is spent visiting air displays all over Europe to display the A10. Like all the USAF display aircraft he has a back-up machine with him to cover any temporary snags that might arise with the number one aircraft. A full engineering team together with boxes of spares also follow the display aircraft. This is a highly professional and very expensive undertaking but it ensures that the USAF is always able to perform.

The British Airways "aerobatic" 737 display flown by Capt. Ian McGrath performed high and low speed passes. This was followed by Richard Goode and his Pitts who brought the action up to a two minute break while the Red Arrows team manager, Polish born Sqn. Ldr. Henry Ploszek, who also acted as team commentator, set the scene for the Red Arrows 88th display of the 1987 season. Formed in 1965 they had now given over 2,000 displays world wide, first flying nine red Gnats before re-equipping with the two seater Hawk, an advanced jet trainer which is powered by a Rolls Royce Ardour engine giving a maximum speed of 572 knots. The nine arrows routed from the RAF base in Valley, North Wales. At 14.30 hrs. there was a sudden whoosh as they came over the Dublin mountains trailing red, white and blue smoke in the big nine forma-

93 Aer Turas DC8

94 Ryanair BAC1-11

95 B-17 with USAF A-10

96 Red Arrows over Baldonnel

tion. Team leader Sqn. Ldr. Richard Thomas then gave the call "Diamond Go" to his team while Ploszek made his historic announcement "Ladies and gentlemen, I present the Red Arrows". From that moment any apprehension we might have felt about the Red Arrows appearing at Baldonnel instantly disappeared as the synchro pair drew a heart shape in the sky with smoke and the remaining seven in arrow formation dived through it. Gerry O'Hare reporting for the *Irish Press* remarked that the crowds responded with huge applause and a shout went up, "we love you too", as they stared skywards in amazement. Thousands of Irish hearts were won over by the most professional aerobatic team in the world. The Red Arrows present a consistently safe yet most entertaining display. Aviation enthusiasts over from England reported that the sustained and spontaneous applause was a reaction unheard of among British audiences. The commentator had barely time for a quick handshake and congratulations before departing in his Jetstream aircraft to follow the Arrows to the next display of the day at Jurby in the Isle of Man.

Pop star Gary Numan then took to the air in his Harvard painted to represent a Japanese Zero. He spotted a twin engined light transport aircraft and went in to attack. Soon the transport disappeared behind the trees belching smoke from one engine. Gary soon came under attack himself from Anthony Hutton leading his section of escorting Harvards. The Zero darted away for cover also trailing smoke. Gary Numan, a dedicated aviation enthusiast, had joined the Harvard formation team in 1985. The aerial attack sequence proved very popular with the audience.

Making a most unusual shape in the sky was the PBY 5A Catalina World War One flying boat as it approached the airfield from Killiney. One of the most famous flying boats in aviation history this particular Catalina had been operated for only the last two seasons in the European airshow circuit and was still capable of landing on either land or sea. After displaying it went to the static aircraft park where spectators could walk through the historic aircraft and talk to pilot Flt. Lt. John Watts who is one of the people responsible for bringing the Catalina to Europe.

Capt. Kevin Byrne on commentary set the scene for the Irish Air Corps display from their home base and cradle of Irish aviation. The highlight which attracted very favourable comment was the skilled display by the four Fouga Magister jets, dubbed the "silver swallows", who flew formation loops, rolls and heart stopping opposition passes, all without the benefit of smoke to heighten their manoeuvres. The audience were well nigh punch drunk with the high quality aerial action but there was more to come. Aer Lingus displayed the first aircraft to join their fleet in 1936, the "Iolar" (Eagle) and the latest, the 360 commuter which was position-

97 Gary Numan and his "Zero"

98 Robin Bowes in the Fokker Triplane

ing for static display before collecting a party of handicapped scouts to return to Dublin Airport.

The Air Atlantique DC3 carried thirty six Irish parachutists aloft to begin the annual colourful invasion of silk from the skies above Baldonnel. At a height of 8,000 ft. it dropped the first eighteen skydivers in freefall to 2,000 ft. before opening their chutes. On the second run twelve jumpers exited followed by the four man international team Tony Sheehan, Trish Reynolds, Kevin Fortune and Nicky Nelson who linked their deployed parachutes together in a four way stack, each parachutist standing on the other's shoulders. The final exit was the first public display of a tandem parachute in Ireland. Joe Bassett was carrying Eunan Carroll as passenger under the enlarged canopy. Because of the larger wing area the chute took a long time to come down. As it descended gracefully there was an amusing exchange between commentator Mike Kelly on the PA and Joe in the air. Mike urged him to hurry up and land as there was an F-16 in the air, a little short of fuel and getting very anxious about the delay. The tandem jumpers made a beautiful landing to appreciative applause from the crowd.

Capt. John Hartke then brought in the F-16 which was enroute to another display and started with a touch and go before moving into splits, rolls, spirals and other manoeuvres. This is a +9G machine and Hartke worked hard for our enjoyment. Grace the Ace, who in real life is sixty year old Grace Tinsley from Palm Beach, California, took to the air in a borrowed Piper Cub and performed stunts which left us all with our hearts in our mouths. She had telexed a few months earlier that she was coming to Ireland on a visit in August and would be happy to do her air display turn at Air Spectacular. On checking I found that she had been performing on the American circuit for twenty years, had started flying at the age of fifteen and in 1978 had set a world record at Tucson, Arizona by spinning her Piper Cub eighty two times in a dive from 10,000 ft. to 2,500 ft. At Baldonnel she performed her comedy act and car chase pretending to be a frail old lady learning to fly with a little help from the commentary to set the scene. The Cub's owner Eddie O'Loughlin from Monasterevin was happy to see his aircraft still in one piece at the end of Grace the Ace's routine.

Brendan O'Brien and Mac Maiklam driving an Iveco trailer truck then featured one of the most novel and exciting display acts for the 1987 air display season and only performed for the first time in June. Mac set off down the runway keeping a steady speed of 60 mph. Brendan, already aloft in his Piper Cub, approached at 100 mph. and lined up on the forty foot trailer with specially reinforced roof to support the Cub and two wheel wells with clamps to secure the aircraft's undercarriage on

99 Catalina Flying Boat

landing. Mac was in radio contact with Brendan and followed the air-craft's approach via a video camera mounted on the cab roof. As there was a stiff breeze blowing across the runway the line up was tricky because the platform provided the wheels with only three inches clearance on either side. After a few attempts it was beginning to look as though the weather conditions were against him. Certainly he had tried hard and the crowd had got its thrills just seeing Brendan attempting the impos-sible. One final approach and then success. He was down and safely locked in the wheel clamps. A roar of approval erupted from the crowd who were with him all the way. After doing a lap of honour on top of the truck it was time to separate again. Mac accelerated down the runway. The Cub reached lift off speed, Brendan pulled back the stick, the air-craft lifted but one of the wheel clamps failed to release cleanly. Disaster was seconds away. The Cub rolled to the right and frantically clawed back into the air as the clamp relented and allowed the wheel its freedom.

The Cub turned right and climbed away, dipping its wings to the crowd. Relaxing in the caravan with us later Brendan admitted it was a close shave. He collected his well earned fee and the two set off for a week's tour of Ireland in the Piper Cub, including a first visit to the Aran Islands.

The French military parachute display team "Equipe Phoenix" one of the final acts of the day gave an outstanding descent with colourful canopies and smoke. USAF F-15 flown by Major John Voss provided the contrast. Then the happy and thoroughly entertained crowds headed home with very few delays reported. Many and glowing letters were received during the next few weeks. Among other things, it became clear from these that the star performer on the ground was the new toilet block.

Air Spectacular '87 was the kind of display I had worked long and hard to organise. The show had finally reached the heights that Tom Hudson and I knew it was capable of reaching. Over the years the team had become a thoroughly professional group of amateurs. It was a wonderful reward to have helped the show to grow from a small event at Fairyhouse back in 1978 to one of the top airshows on the international air calendar. Thanks to the team and our sponsor Aer Rianta, Air Spectacular now stands proudly among the very best air displays anywhere.

Two pieces of advice were given to me over the years by those who should know. My father, Peter Byrne, an engineer, always preached the sound philosophy that "if you set out to do something then do it as well as you can". My grandfather Bill Poole a great sportsman in his own right had coached my mother Olive in tennis and she went on to represent Ireland at Wimbledon just before the war. He had served on many sporting committees over the years and always maintained that one should stop when one is ahead. I have applied the first piece of advice during my ten years as show co-ordinator and I decided to take the second at the end of Air Spectacular '87 which was the year it all came right for us. It was time to retire gracefully.

The enjoyment that Air Spectacular has given me and the many friendships I have made far outweigh the thousands of hours of hard slog that went into its preparation. I wish the show well. It will always be very much a part of me, the experiences, the successes, the failures, the happy and the sad moments and of course the people and the showmen who made it great. I have been privileged to meet some interesting, hard working and courageous people.

This show has ended but the next is just beginning. If you have not been to one yet then please visit an airshow. You don't know what you are missing *but do come early*. See you in the crowd sometime.

100 Pat Kenny interviews USAF pilots Sean Jessurn and John Voss

101 Joe Bassett in freefall

Appendix 1

The Irish Aviation Council and Sport Aviation

The IAC which is the present controlling body for sport aviation in Ireland can trace its roots back to 1909 when the Aero Club of Ireland was established to promote and encourage the new and exciting era of flight. The Aero Club of Ireland ceased operations at the beginning of World War One.

The Irish Aero Club was founded in August 1928 and its aim was to ensure the development of civil aviation in Ireland. The chairman was Col. Fitzmaurice. The club operated from Baldonnel and offered the first civil registered aircraft in the Irish Free State for tuition. It organised many displays in the 1930s in conjunction with Cobham and other aviators. The Irish Aero Club was wound up at the end of 1937.

The Irish Aviation Club was formed on 15 April 1946 with a similar mandate which included the promotion of sport aviation in all its forms. The first president was Sean O hUadhaig, chairman of Aer Lingus and vice presidents included Sean Lemass TD, Captain J.C. Kelly Rogers OBE and Colonel Charles Russell. The honorary secretary was Chris Bruton and Denis Greene was honorary treasurer. Five aero clubs were affiliated and the Model Aeronautics Council was represented on the board.

In September 1946 club delegate Denis Greene travelled to London to attend the general conference of the world controlling body for sport aviation, the Federation Aeronautique Internationale. Ireland was admitted as a member at this meeting.

By 1950 financial constraints meant that private aviation in Ireland had great difficulty in keeping active. The number of flying clubs was reduced to one. In 1955 the Irish Aviation Club became a limited company and under the guidance of Capt. J.C. Kelly Rogers and secretary G.H. Giltrap, representatives of powered flying, gliding and aero modelling were formed into new sub-committees and an overall policy was formulated for the development and promotion of sporting aviation in Ireland.

Many new aviation sports were encouraged and flourished under the IAC's guidance and financial aid. Attendance at international competitive aviation events was encouraged as was the organisation of events in Ireland. An interest free loan scheme was set up with the assistance of Aer Rianta, the Irish airports authority, to encourage flying clubs to purchase their own training aircraft. This scheme helped many clubs to become established over the years and fulfilled that part of Aer Rianta's charter which requires it to assist in the development and promotion of aviation.

In 1973 the IAC hosted the 66th World general conference of the FAI in Dublin. Guided by club president, Dr. Colm Killeen, vice-president Terry Rowan and secretary C.P. Martin, the delegates from sixty-four countries were treated to the best of Irish hospitality. Among the distinguished guests were astronauts John Young and Eugene Cernan who received FAI awards. The IAC also presented specially struck medals to mark the occasion.

In August 1978 the IAC organised its first Air Spectacular at Fairyhouse to raise funds for and to act as showcase for sporting aviation.

The Irish Aviation Club changed its name to Irish Aviation Council in 1979. It was felt that this name would be more descriptive of its role today.

The council today is made up of representatives from the affiliated bodies. Two elected representatives from each of the affiliated sports sit on the board of the council at its monthly meetings. An annual general meeting is held at which officers and delegates are elected. All of the aviation sports are represented as are the Air Education Council, the Irish Aviation Museum, Aviation Medicine and Air Scouts. A representative from the Department of Defence also sits on the board. All positions are honorary and voluntary.

The council in turn is affiliated to the FAI which is an international body made up of the various national aero clubs and which controls private and sporting flying worldwide. The FAI is the organisation which lays down the conditions for attaining flying records of various kinds and it supervises these attempts.

The IAC does not control individual clubs but allows all sports to come together to present the united voice of sport aviation in Ireland.

Irish Aviation Council Members 1988

Model Aeronautics Council of Ireland	founded 1936
Irish Gliding Association	reformed 1960
Aircraft Owners and Pilots Association	founded 1967
Dublin Ballooning Club	founded 1968
Irish Sport Parachute Association	founded 1973
Irish Hang Gliding Association	founded 1974
Society of Amateur Aircraft Constructors	founded 1978
Irish Microlight Aircraft Association	founded 1980
National Aerobatics Club of Ireland	founded 1982
Precision Flying Association	founded 1986

Appendix 2

Air Spectacular 1978 Fairyhouse
Sunday 27 August

SNCAN Stampe SV.4C Aerobatics	G-AYWT	Brian Lecomber
Model Aircraft Control Line Flying		
Parachute Drop Aer Arran Islander BN2A	EI-AWM	
Glider Rigging Race		
Crazy Flying Routine – Stampe SV.4C	G-AYWT	Brian Lecomber
Aer Lingus 737 Flypast		
Aer Arran Islander Demonstration BN2A	EI-AWM	Capt. Paddy Robinson
Irish Air Corps Alouette Rescue	214	
Morane MS.894A Minerva 220	EI-AYT	
Model Aircraft Radio Control Flying		
Golly Hot Air Balloon	G-OLLI	Tom Sage
Dublin Ballooning Club Hot Air Balloon		
Cameron 0.65	EI–BBM	David Hooper
Homebuilt Evans VP1	EI-AYY	John O'Loughlin
Hang Glider Drop from Hot Air Balloon	EI-BAN	Mike Alexander
Cameron 0.65		John Harris
Airwork Agusta-Bell AB 206 B Helicopter	EI-BEV	

Air Spectacular 1979 Fairyhouse
Sunday 26 August

Cessna 414 Flypast	EI-AWW	John Coltan
British Airways Rapide DH89A	G-AKOE	
Prizewinners of Timed Arrival Competition		
Flypast		
Morane MS.893A Commodore 180	EI-AWJ	Bill Phelan
Parachute Star Formation Free Fall from DC3C	EI-BDU	
Air Corps Display		
– Alouette	196	
– Marchetti	230	
– Fouga Jets	216 218	
	219 220	
Aer Arran Islander BN.2A	EI-AWM	Capt. Paddy Robinson
Glider Rigging Race D.G.C. v I.H.G.A.		
Gliding Display		
Model Aircraft Radio Control & Control Line		
Bücker Jungmeister 133C Aerobatics	G-AXIH	Roy Legge
British Airways Model 747 Jumbo Take Off		
Airwork Crop Spraying Demonstration		

Augusta-Bell AB.206B Helicopter		
	EI-BHE	
Flightlines Rockwell 690B	EI-BGL	Tony Doyle
Morane-Saulnier MS 230	EI-ARG	Capt. John Hutchinson
Powered Hang Glider		Jim Potts
British Airways Rapide DH89A	G-AKOE	Sq. Ldr. Dick Milliard
Clyden Airlines DC3C Flypast	EI-BDU	
Homebuilt Evans VP1	EI-AYY	John O'Loughlin
Homebuilt Tipsy Nipper III	G-AVKK	
Hang Glider Drop from Hot Air Balloon	EI-BAN	Mike Alexander/
Cameron 0.65		John Harris
Hot Air Balloon Race		
— Cameron 0.65	EI-BBM	Colm O'Rourke
— Colt 77A	EI-BGT	Kevin Haugh
— Cameron AX8-84	EI-BAY	Noel Lewis
Aerobatics	G-AXIH	Roy Legge

Air Spectacular 1980 Fairyhouse
Sunday 17 August

Aviamilano F8L Falco 3 Aerobatics	EI-BBT	Capt. Neil Johnson
Irish Parachutists (35) Drop from Clyden DC3C	EI-BDT	
Air Corps Display		
— Gazelle	237	
— Marchetti	222 225	
	226 228	
— Alouette Rescue Demo	212	
Homebuilt Aircraft		
— Evans VP.1 No 2	EI-BBD	Brendan Feeley
— Evans VP1 MD.1	EI-AYY	John O'Loughlin
Avair Beech King Air 200	{ EI-BHA,	
Flypast	(EI-BIP,	
Beechcraft 77 Skipper	{ EI-BHT,	
Flypast	(EI-BHU	
Vampire DH.115 T11	G-VT11	John Turnbull
Model Aircraft Display		
Gliding Display Irish Gliding Association		
Iona National Airlines Flypast		
— Cessna F172N	EI-BCK	
— Cessna F337F	EI-AVC	
— Cessna 310Q	EI-BEO	
— Cessna 414A	EI-BGP	Peter Cahill
Gyroplane Campbell Cricket	G-AXVK	John Kitchin
Powered Glider Schleicher ASK.16	EI-AYR	Stanley Dunne
B.17 Flying Fortress Sally B	G-BEDF	
Skytrike & MASH Jeep — Novelty Item		
Parachute Drop from Islander BN 2A	EI-BCE	
Flightlines Rockwell 690B	EI-BGL	
Airwork Aerial Spraying Demonstration from		
Helicopter Augusta-Bell 47G-3B-1	G-BEHL	

Air Spectacular 1981 Fairyhouse
Sunday 16 August

Pitts S2A Special	EI-BKA	Arthur Wignall
Harvard T-6 J Texan	G-BGPB	Ray Pullan
Piper Super Cub 180 Short Take Off Demo	EI-BIK	Dan Begley
Air Corps Display		
— Fouga Magisters	215 218	
	219 220	
— Gazelle	241 237	K. Byrne/F. Condon
— Alouettes	213 214	
SNCAN Stampe SV.4C	EI-BLB	John Hutchinson
Parachute Drop		
Model Aircraft Display		
CL-44J Aer Turas	EI-BGO	Capt. Mike Green
Weston School Fly Past		Capt. Darby Kennedy
Gyrocopter Bensen B.8M	G-ARWW	
Gliding Display		
Homebuilt Aircraft		
Avair Fly Past		
— Beech 77 Skipper	EI-BHT	
— Beech 77 Skipper	EI-BHU	
— King Air 200	EI-BJY	
Microlight Skytrike		
Aer Arran Islander BN.2A	EI-AWM	Capt. Paddy Robinson
Dunlop Pitts Special	G-BOOK	Brian Lecomber
Parascending Demonstration		
Mass Hot Air Balloon Ascent		
— Cameron V.56	G-BEND	
— Cameron 0.65	EI-BBM	David Hooper
— Cameron AX8.84	EI-BAY	
— Cameron Special Shape	G-PNUT	
— Colt 77A	EI-BGT	Kevin Haugh
Hang Glider & Parachute Drop from Balloons	M. McManus/N. Duignan	

Air Spectacular 1982 Fairyhouse
Sunday 22 August

Rothmans Vixen Two Pitts S2A	G-BDKS	John McClean
	G-BECM	Marcus Edwards
Gliding Display		
Avair Shorts SD330 Fly Past	EI-BLP	Capt. Henk Van Der Zee
Air Corps Display		
— Alouette Rescue Demo	202	
— Gazelle & Puma Helicopters	241 242	
— Four Fouga Magister Formation	216 217	
	218 219	
— King Air	234 240	

Autogyro "Little Nellie" WA.116	G-ARZB	Wing Comd. Wallis
Hawker F51 Hunter Jet	G-HUNT	Adrien Gjertsen
Irish Parachute Drop from 748		
BAe HS 748 – 2A Touch and Go	G-BDVH	
RF-4C Phantom USAF	68-570	
YAK C-11	G-AYAK	Anthony Hutton
F-111s (2) USAF		
Flightlines Rockwell 690B	EI-BGL	Capt. Tony Doyle
Iona Banner Tow		
Iona Cessna 310Q & 414A	EI-BEO	
	EI-BGP	
Weston Rallye Minerva 220 MS.894A	EI-AUG	
Weston Socata Tampico TB9	EI-BMI	
F-15C Eagles (4) USAF	79.046,	
	79.062,	
	80.002,	
	80.018	
Harp Pitts S2A	EI-BKA	Capt. Arthur Wignall
Model Aircraft Display		
Bandeirante Air Ecosse EMB110P2	G-DATA	
HH53C Super Jolly Helicopter USAF	95784	Capt. Bobdube

Air Spectacular 1983 Fairyhouse
Sunday 21 August

C-141B Starlifter		
Pace Spirit Aerobatic Display	G-OODO	Richard Goode
Harvard AT6-4	G-BIWX	Anthony Hutton
Gliding Display		
Mass Parachute Drop Shorts Skyvan	EI-BNN	
British Aerospace Jetstream	G-BKHI	
Spitfire XIV	G-FIRE	Chris Bevin
Air Corps Display		
— BAe HS 125 Executive Jet	238	
— Maritime King Air	232	
— Marchetti	222 223	
	228 229	
— Gazelle	241	
— Alouettes	202 213	
— Fouga Magister	215 216	
	220	
Avair Shorts SD.330	EI-BLP	
Autogyro "Little Nellie" WA 116	G-ARZB	Wing Comd. Wallis
A10 Thunderbolt USAF	80-231	
	81-964	
	81-987	
Aer Arran Islander BN.2A	EI-AYN	Paddy Robinson
Model Aircraft Display		
Slingsby Firefly T.67M	G-SFTZ	Norrie Grove

Harp Pitts S2A	EI-BKA	Arthur Wignall
Vixen 3 Pitts S2A/S2E/S2A	G-BECM,	Andy Wallbridge
	G-BKTC	John McClean
	G-BADY	Marcus Edwards
Helio Super Courier H.295	EI-BNE	Des McCarthy
HH53 Sikorsky Super Jolly Helicopter USAF	95784	
Hot Air Balloons		
— Colt 17A Smirnoff one man balloon	G-BJXD	Colin Prescot
— Cameron 0.65 D.B.C.	EI-BBM	David Hooper
Microlights		
— Southern Puma Lightning	EI-BMR	Tom Hudson
— Ultrasports Puma 440	G-MJGY	John Byrne

Air Spectacular 1984 Fairyhouse
Sunday 12 August

Vixen Solo Pitts S2A	G-BDKS	Marcus Edwards
Rutan Long Ez	G-RAFT	Don Foreman
Evans VP1	EI-AYY	John O'Loughlin
Harvards		
— AT 6-4	G-BIWX	
— AT 6C	G-BGOU	
— AT 6C	G-TEAC	
— AT-16 IIB	G-BDAM	
Air Corps Display		
— Alouette	211	Harvey O'Keefe
— Marchetti	223 227	
	228 231	
— Gazelle	237 241	P. Fry/D. Cotter
— King Air	232 234	
	240	
— Super Magister (solo)	219	Dermot McCarthy
Parachute Drop from Shorts Skyvan	EI-BNN	
French Air Force Alpha Jet	E.159	Lt. Bourlard
Valmet L-70	OH-VAA	Hannu Halonen
Powered Gliders Fournier RF4D	G-AVNZ	John Taylor
	G-AVLW	Brendan O'Brien
F-15C Eagles USAF	79.029	
	81.048	
Aer Lingus Commuter Shorts SD 360	EI-BEM	Capt. Tom Croke
PZL 104 Wilgas	SP-AFV	Vitold Sviadek
	SP-AFX	Jan Baran
	SP-AFZ	Chris Lenartovicz
F-111E USAF	68.041	
Dunlop Pitts S1	G-BOOK	Brian Lecomber
RF-4C Phantom USAF	68-555	
Comper Swift CLA7	G-ABTC	Pete Channon
Aer Turas CL-44J	EI-BGO	Capt. Nigel Budd
F-16A USAF	80.563	Major Alain Kamerer

Gliding Display Irish Gliding Association
Aer Arran Islander BN2A   EI-AYN   Capt. Paddy Robinson
Smirnoff Cloudship (Colt AS.42 Airship)   G-WZZZ   Ian Ashpole

Air Spectacular 1985 Cork
Planned list of events for Sunday 18 August

Arrival and Departure Aer Lingus, British Airways, Dan Air
Brymon Air, Brit Air and Manx Airways flights
Parachute Spotting Competition
Banner Tow
Joy Rides by Air Atlantique DC3 and Irish Helicopters
Aerobatics Display — Richard Goode
Air Corps Display — Fougas, Gazelles and Alouettes
Mass Parachute Drop
DC3 Displays by Air Atlantique and Hibernian
007 Autogyro "Little Nellie" — Wing Commander Wallis
B-17 Flying Fortress Sally B
F-16, F-15, F-111 USAF
Powered Glider — Fournier Duo Aerobatic Display
Microlight Display
Homebuilt Aircraft Display
F-104 Starfighters — German Navy Vikings Display Team
Alpha Jet — French Air Force
Beech 18 — Anthony Hutton
Gliding Display — Dublin Gliding Club
HH53 Sikorsky Super Jolly Helicopter USAF
Frecci Tricolori Aerobatic Team — Italian Air Force
Model Aircraft — Control Line and Radio Control
BAC 1-11
Hot Air Balloons

Air Spectacular 1986 Baldonnel
Sunday 17 August

Iona Triple Banner Tow
Rallye Club Trainer   Capt. Darby Kennedy
British Airways 737   G-BKYL   Capt. Ian McGrath
Pitts Special S1   G-OODI   Richard Goode
F-16 USAF   84-1326   Major Beltz
DH98 Mosquito TT. MK.35   G-ASKH   Tony Craig
Spitfire IX   G-LFIX   Nick Grace
Air Corps Display
  — Reims Cessna 172s   203 205
                                 206 243
  — Dauphin   244 245
                                 246

— Marchetti	222 225	
	226 230	
— Beech King Air	234	
— BAe 125-700	238	
— Alouette	212	
— Gazelle	241	
Aer Turas CL-44J	EI-BRP	Capt. Nigel Budd
DH 115 Vampire T.11	G-VTII	Stan Hodgkins
Phenix French Air Force Parachute Drop		
Nord Noratlas French Air Force	96/63-VH	
Alpha Jet French Air Force	E22/314	Lt. Philip Cartigniers
Aer Lingus DH 84 Dragon II "Iolar"	EI-ABI	Capt. J.J. Sullivan
Gliding Display Irish Gliding Association		
RF-4C Phantom USAF	69-0372	
Irish Helicopters Sikorsky S.61N	EI-BHO	
Gates Learjet	N457JA	
BAe HS 125-800B	G-TSAM	
Air Atlantique DC4 Dakota	G-AMPY	
MB339 Italian Air Force	MM 54535	Major Andrea Canetto
Fokker DR1 Triplane (Replica)	G-BEFR	Robin Bowes
Grumman Widgeon	N444M	Michael Dunkerly
British Aerospace Jetstream 3100	G-BLHC	
Fournier Powered Gliders RF4D	G-AVWY	Tizi Hodson
	G-AVNZ	John Taylor
Partenavia P.68B	G-OBSV	

Air Spectacular 1987 Baldonnel
Sunday 16 August

F-16s USAF	85-400	
	85-440	
	85-454	
	85-459	
Aer Lingus 747 St. Patrick	EI-ASJ	
Aer Turas DC8 — 63CF	EI-BNA	
Ryan Air BAC 1-11	EI-BSY	Capt. Mike O'Brien
Decathlon Bellanca 9KCAB	EI-BIV	Peter Hynes
Aer Arran Islander BN.2A	EI-AYN	Capt. Paddy Robinson
B17 Flying Fortress Sally B	G-BEDF	Keith Sissons
A 10 Thunderbolt USAF	81-952	Capt. Sean Jessurn
Irish Helicopters S.61N	EI-BHO	
British Airways 737	G-BKYC	Capt. Ian McGrath
Pitts S1	G-OODI	Richard Goode
Red Arrows Aerobatic Team RAF Hawks	XX243	
	XX252	
	XX253	
	XX259	
	XX260	
	XX264	

	XX266	
	XX304	
	XX227	
British Aerospace Jetstream 3102	G-BKKY	
Gliding Display Irish Gliding Association		
Catalina PBY-5A	G-BLSC	Fl. Lt. John Watts
Harvards Attack Sequence		
— IIB AT-16	G-AZSC	Gary Numan
— IIB AT-16	G-BDAM	Anthony Hutton
— AT6C	G-TEAC	
Beech 18	N5063N	
Weston Rallye 100ST Display	EI-BBJ	Capt. Darby Kennedy
Air Corps Display		
— Fouga Magisters (silver swallows)	216 217	
	219 220	
— Beech King Air	234 240	
— BAe 125-700	238	
— Cessna 172	206	
— Dauphin	245	
— Marchetti	226	
— Gazelle	237	
Aer Lingus DH84 Dragon II "Iolar"	EI-ABI	
Aer Lingus Commuter Shorts SD.360	EI-BPD	
Rutan Long Ez	G-WILY	
Wallis WA 116 Autogyro "Little Nellie"	G-ARZB	Wing Comd. Wallis
Irish Parachute Association Jump		
From DC4 Dakota	G-AMSV	
F-16 USAF	82-1002	Capt. John Hartke
Club Air 727	EI-BUI	
Grace the Ace (Piper Super Cub 95)	EI-ANY	Grace Tinsley
Robin ATL	F-GFSZ	
Phenix French Air Force Parachute Team		
DHC6/6 Twin Otter	742/65-CB	
Truck Top Landing (Piper Super Cub 150)	G-BLMR	Brendan O'Brien
F-15 Eagle USAF	79-45	Major John Voss
Snowbird 77DS		Marcus Edwards

Cobham Tour 1933 July

Saturday	1	Kildonan Finglas Dublin
Sunday	2	Kildonan Finglas Dublin
Monday	3	Waterford
Tuesday	4	Clonmel
Wednesday	5	Cork Ballincollig Aerodrome
Thursday	6	Cork Ballincollig Aerodrome
Friday	7	Limerick Ballycummin Castle — Crash
Saturday	8	Limerick Ballycummin Castle
Sunday	9	Kildonan Finglas Dublin

Monday	10	Galway Oranmore Aerodrome
Tuesday	11	Bundoran
Wednesday	12	Londonderry
Thursday	13	Londonderry
Friday	14	Belfast
Saturday	15	Belfast
Sunday	16	Dundalk
Monday	17	Depart for England

Cobham Tour 1933 September/October

Tuesday	12	Carlow Ballybar
Wednesday	13	Wexford Killiane
Thursday	14	Dungarvan Ballinamuck
Friday	15	Fermoy Aerodrome
Saturday	16	Athy Cardenton
Sunday	17	Dublin Portmarnock
Monday	18	Boyle Ballymore
Tuesday	19	Bundoran Ellesmere Park
Wednesday	20	Sligo Scardenmore
Thursday	21	Castlebar Old Aerodrome
Friday	22	Ballinrobe Racecourse
Saturday	23	Nenagh Rathnaleen
Sunday	24	Killarney Western Park
Monday	25	Tralee Ballinorig
Tuesday	26	Newcastle West Dongeeha
Wednesday	27	Mallow Racecourse
Thursday	28	Cahir Kilcommon
Friday	29	Tullamore Kinnity Road
Saturday	30	Athlone The Big Meadow
Sunday	1	Drogheda Colpe Farm
Monday	2	Depart for England

Cobham National Aviation Display 1935 May

Friday	3	Carlow Ballybar
Saturday	4	Enniscorthy Hollyfort
Sunday	5	Dundalk Marsh Farm
Monday	6	Belfast
Tuesday	7	Belfast
Wednesday	8	Coleraine
Thursday	9	Londonderry
Friday	10	Sligo Scardenmore
Saturday	11	Dublin Leopardstown
Sunday	12	Dublin Phoenix Park
Monday	13	Maryborough Bloomfield
Tuesday	14	Wexford Drinagh
Wednesday	15	Kilkenny Dunmore

Thursday	16	Waterford Kilcohan Park Racecourse
Friday	17	Limerick Ballycummin Castle
Saturday	18	Cork Farmers Cross Aerodrome
Sunday	19	Cork Farmers Cross Aerodrome
Monday	20	Tralee Racecourse
Tuesday	21	Galway Oranmore Aerodrome
Wednesday	22	Castlebar Old Aerodrome
Thursday	23	Athlone Big Meadow
Friday	24	Longford Clooncoose Racecourse

Scott Circus Timetable 1936

Sunday	10	May	Phoenix Park Dublin
Monday	11	May	Raheny Dublin (near railway station)
Tuesday	12	May	Maryborough
Wednesday	13	May	Longford
Thursday	14	May	Athlone
Friday	15	May	Thurles
Saturday	16	May	Cobh
Sunday	17	May	Cork Farmers Cross
Monday	18	May	Dungarvan
Tuesday	19	May	Mallow
Wednesday	20	May	Fermoy Aerodrome
Thursday	21	May	Clonmel
Friday	22	May	Tralee
Saturday	23	May	Newcastle West
Sunday	24	May	Limerick Banemore Ballycummin
Monday	25	May	Kilkenny
Tuesday	26	May	Arklow
Wednesday	27	May	Wexford
Thursday	28	May	Waterford
Friday	29	May	Wicklow Kilpoole
Saturday	30	May	Dundalk
Sunday	31	May	Drogheda
			To Northern Ireland
Sunday	7	June	Sligo
Monday	8	June	Boyle
Tuesday	9	June	Castlebar
Wednesday	10	June	Ballinrobe
Thursday	11	June	Galway
Friday	12	June	Ennis Castleclare
Saturday	13	June	Tuam
Sunday	14	June	Nenagh
Monday	15	June	Naas
Tuesday	16	June	Enniscorthy Hollyfort House
Wednesday	17	June	Carlow
Thursday	18	June	Leopardstown Racecourse Dublin

Air Demonstrations Ltd. Tour 1937
Under the auspices of the Irish Aero Club with Irish Press

From Northern Ireland

Sunday	30	May	Dublin Phoenix Park
Monday	31	May	Drogheda
Tuesday	1	June	Longford The Racecourse Clooncoose
Wednesday	2	June	Maryborough Ballymoney (Portlaoise)
Thursday	3	June	Carlow Ballybar Lower
Friday	4	June	Clonmel Abbeyfarm
Saturday	5	June	Dungarvan
Sunday	6	June	Tipperary Town Rathnaveen
Monday	7	June	Mitchelstown Broomhill
Tuesday	8	June	Kilkenny Dunmore
Wednesday	9	June	Enniscorthy Hollyfort
Thursday	10	June	Waterford Kilcohan Park
Friday	11	June	Thurles Lognafulla
Saturday	12	June	Newcastle West
Sunday	13	June	Limerick Bawnmore
Monday	14	June	Limerick Bawnmore
Tuesday	15	June	Portarlington Tierhogar
Wednesday	16	June	Nenagh The Racecourse Lisbunny
Thursday	17	June	Ennis Clarecastle Claremount Farm
Friday	18	June	Roscommon Munsborough
Saturday	19	June	Tuam The Racecourse
Sunday	20	June	Galway Oranmore Aerodrome
Monday	21	June	Ballinrobe The Racecourse
Tuesday	22	June	Mullingar Newbrook Racecourse
Wednesday	23	June	Sligo Scardenmore
Thursday	24	June	Ballinsloe Ashford
Friday	25	June	Naas Lewistown
Monday	28	June	Skerries Balcunnin
Tuesday	29	June	Wicklow Kilpoole
Wednesday	30	June	Arklow
Thursday	1	July	Athy
Friday	2	July	Cahir Kilcommon The Parade Field
Saturday	3	July	New Ross Tinnaranny
Sunday	4	July	Wexford
Monday	5	July	Thomastown Jerpoint Hill
Tuesday	6	July	Lismore Ballymartin Tullow Road
Wednesday	7	July	Castletown Roche
Saturday	10	July	Cobh Belvelly
Sunday	11	July	Mitchelstown Co. Cork
Monday	12	July	Killorglin
Tuesday	13	July	Kanturk Ballyheen
Wednesday	14	July	Kilmallock
Thursday	15	July	Rathluirc Charleville

also displays in Templemore, Roscrea, Birr and Mallow

Bibliography

Baker, John A. and Bish, Peter J., *British Balloons*, London 1981.

Bramson and Birch, *The Tiger Moth Story*, Airlife, Shrewsbury 1982.

Butler, P.H., *Irish Aircraft*, Merseyside Aviation Society, Liverpool 1972.

Byrne, Liam, *History of Aviation in Ireland*, Blackwater, Dublin 1980.

Cobham, Sir Alan J., *A Time to Fly*, Shepheard Walwyn, London 1978.

Corbett Wilson, Denys, *Aviation's Forgotten Pioneer*, Paul Williams, Pembrokeshire 1987.

Corlett, John, *Aviation in Ulster*, Blackstaff Press, Belfast 1981.

Cunniffe, P., Hayes, K., Power E., *Flying Fields of Cork*, Irish Air Letter, Dublin 1988.

Cunniffe, P., Hayes, K., Power, E., *Aviation on the Shannon*, Irish Air Letter, Dublin 1985.

F.A.I., *The F.A.I. Annual Bulletins*, F.A.I., Paris.

Gillian and Cooke, *The Red Arrows*, Planet, London 1987.

Gwynn-Jones, Terry, *The Air Racers 1909-1936*, Guild, London, 1983.

Hooper and O'Rourke, *10th Anniversary Dublin Ballooning Club*, D.B.C., Dublin 1978.

Jackson, A.J., *British Civil Aircraft Vols. 1, 2, 3*, Putnam, London, 1973.

Janes, *Encyclopedia of Aviation*, Janes, London 1980.

Jerram, Michael, *Biplanes*, Michael Joseph, London 1982.

Johnson, Howard, *Wings Over Brooklands*, Whittet Books, London 1985.

Kniveton, Gordon N., *Manx Aviation in War and Peace*, Isle of Man 1985.

Ogilvy, David, *Flying Displays*, Airlife, Shrewsbury 1984.

Peel, Dave, *British Civil Aircraft Registers Since 1919*, Midland Counties Publications, Leicester 1985.

Quigley, A.A., *Green Is My Sky*, Avoca Publications, Dublin 1983.

R.A.F., *R.A.F. Yearbook 1987 & 1988*, I.A.T. Publishing, London.

Share, Bernard, Flight of the 'Iolar', Gill and Macmillan, Dublin, 1986.

Smallwood, Hugh, *2nd TAF Spitfire – Story of Spitfire ML407*, British Aviation Heritage, 1986.

Smith, Anthony, *The First Five Years*, B.B.A.C., Bristol 1973.

Taylor and Mondey, *Milestones in Flight*, Janes, London 1983.

Scale Aircraft Modelling, The Irish Air Corps, Anthony P. Kearns, 1981.

Periodicals

Aero Ireland, Editor Frazer McMillan 1979-1983, Dublin.

Aeroplane Monthly, Editor Richard T. Riding, Surrey.

Aviation, Editor Colonel Charles Russell, 1935, Dublin

Aviation in Ireland, 1784-1912 Capt. J.C. Kelly Rogers, 1971.

Aviation Ireland, Aviation Society of Ireland.

Aviation Ireland, Vol 1-3, Editor Paul Cunniff, Dublin.

Flarepath, Editor Maymes O'Reilly 1964-1965, Dublin.

Irish Air Letter, History of Irish Aero Club I, II, III, 1988.

Irish Air Letter, Editors Paul Cunniffe, Karl E. Hayes, Eamon C. Power.

Irish Aviator, Editor Paul Duffy.

Kildonan 1933-36, A Memory: Katherine Butler, Old Dublin Society, 1984.

Minutes of I.A.C., Board Meetings 1946-1987.

Newspaper Files, National Library, Pearse Street Library.

Pilot, Editor James Gilbert.

S.V. Furlong Scrapbook, Irish Aviation Museum.

Index

I have moved through the skies in dreamtime
My fingers have touched the clouds
The birds with their wings surround me
Far away from the bustling crowds

The golden rays of the sunbeams
Paint pictures in visible light
I marvel at all this beauty
The wonderful magic of flight

I have drifted through hills and valleys
I have pointed my face to the sky
I have seen great vistas below me
Oh what joy to be able to fly

The big crowds came to Dublin
Over two hundred years ago
To witness the aerial excitement
To see what wasn't seen before

More crowds in 1910
And on to the present day
Families enjoy the atmosphere
of the Annual Air Display

Those lucky enough to have been there
Will understand just what I mean
And why I am writing about it
Mere words to describe such a scene

Where the sun is always shining
And the sky is always blue
Long may those wonderful aviators
Perform for me and you.

Colm O'Rourke